Selections from Walt Whitman and Emily Dickinson

Selections from Walt Whitman and Emily Dickinson

FIFTH EDITION

A SUPPLEMENT TO

The Heath Anthology of American Literature

Volume C

Houghton Mifflin Company
Boston   New York

Publisher: Patricia A. Coryell
Executive Editor: Suzanne Phelps Weir
Sponsoring Editor: Michael Gillespie
Development Editor: Bruce Cantley
Editorial Assistant: Lindsey Gentel
Senior Project Editor: Rosemary Winfield
Editorial Assistant: Jake Perry
Manufacturing Coordinator: Chuck Dutton
Senior Marketing Manager: Cindy Graff Cohen
Marketing Associate: Wendy Thayer

Printed in the U.S.A.

ISBN: 0-618-54247-7

3   4   5   6   7   8   9-CRS-09   08   07

CONTENTS

(For easier cross-referencing, the page numbers in this volume are the same as those in Volume 1 of *The Heath Anthology of American Literature,* Fourth Edition.)

2969   **Emily Dickinson (1830–1886)**

Selections from Walt Whitman and Emily Dickinson

Walt Whitman 1819–1892

The publication of *Leaves of Grass* on or about July 4, 1855, represented a revolutionary departure in American literature. Printed at Whitman's expense, the green, quarto-sized volume bore no author's name. Opposite the title page appeared a daguerreotype engraving of the poet, dressed in workingman's trowsers, a shirt unbuttoned to reveal his undershirt, and a hat cocked casually upon his head. In a rousing Preface, the poet declared America's literary independence, and in verse that rolled freely and dithyrambically across the page, he presented himself as "Walt Whitman, an American, one of the roughs, a kosmos,/Disorderly fleshy and sensual . . . . eating drinking and breeding." Like his poet as common man, Whitman's act of self-naming represented an assault on literary decorum and the Puritan pieties of the New England literary establishment. "It is as if the beasts spoke," wrote the otherwise sympathetic Thoreau.

In the six editions of *Leaves of Grass* that were published between 1855 and 1881, Whitman opened the field of American and ultimately of modern poetry. His subject was not "the smooth walks, trimm'd hedges, poseys and nightingales of the English poets, but the whole orb, with its geologic history, the Kosmos, carrying fire and snow." He was the poet not only of Darwinian evolution, but of the city and the crowd, science and the machine. Presenting himself as a model democrat who spoke as and for rather than apart from the people, Whitman's poet was a breaker of bounds: he was female and male, farmer and factory worker, prostitute and slave, citizen of America and citizen of the world; shuttling between past, present, and future, he was "an acme of things accomplished" and an "encloser of things to be." His songs were songs not only of occupations but of sex and the body. He sang of masturbation, the sexual organs, and the

sexual act; he was one of the first poets to write of the "body electric," of female eroticism, homosexual love, and the anguish of repressed desire.

Puzzled by Whitman's sudden emergence at age 36 in 1855 as the American bard, critics have proposed several explanations: a reading of Emerson, a love affair, a mystic experience, an Oedipal crisis. Considered within the context of his time, however, Whitman's emergence seems neither mystifying nor particularly disconnected from his family background and his early life as radical Democrat, political journalist, and sometime dandy. His mother was an ardent follower of the mystical doctrines of the Quaker preacher Elias Hicks, whom Whitman later described as "the democrat in religion as Jefferson was the democrat in politics." His father was a carpenter who embraced the radical political philosophy of Tom Paine and subscribed to the *Free Enquirer*, edited by Frances Wright and Robert Dale Owen, which sought through the rhetoric of class warfare to unite the grievances of New York City workers in an anticapitalist and anticlerical platform. Raised among eight brothers and sisters whose very names— Andrew Jackson, George Washington, and Thomas Jefferson—bore the inscription of the democratic ideals of his family, Whitman early began to develop a sense of self that was inextricably bound up with the political identity of America.

Although Whitman attended school between 1825 and 1830, he was largely self-educated. During the thirties he served as a printer's apprentice, engaged in local politics, and taught for a few years in Long Island schools. He read voraciously but erratically, attended the theater and the opera, and poked about the antiquities at Dr. Abbott's Egyptian Museum. As editor of the *Aurora* in 1842 and later of the Brooklyn *Daily Eagle* (1846–47), Whitman placed himself at the very center of the political battles over slavery, territorial expansion, the Mexican War, sectionalism, free trade, states' rights, worker strife, and the new market economy. His support for David Wilmot's proposal to forbid the extension of slavery into the new territory led to his being fired as editor of the *Eagle*. Perhaps disillusioned by party politics, he began to experiment with the idea of using poetry as a form of political action. When in his earliest notebook, dated 1847, Whitman breaks for the first time into lines approximating the free verse of *Leaves of Grass*, the lines bear the impress of the slavery issue:

I am the poet of slaves, and of the
    masters of slaves
I am the poet of the body
And I am

Similarly, Whitman's first free verse poems, "Blood Money," "House of Friends," and "Resurgemus," which were published in 1850, emerged out of the political passions aroused by slavery, free soil, and the European revolutions of 1848.

Although Whitman continued to support the cause of Free Soil, in the early Fifties he withdrew from party politics. Working part-time as a house builder in Brooklyn, he completed his 1855 edition of *Leaves of Grass*. The poems are propelled by the desire to enlighten and regenerate the people in the ideals of the democratic republic. The drama of identity in the initially untitled "Song of Myself," the first and longest poem in the 1855 *Leaves*, is rooted in the political drama of a nation in crisis. The poet's conflict between separate person and en masse, between pride and sympathy, individualism and equality, nature and the city, the body and the soul, symbolically enacts the larger political conflicts in the nation, which grew out of the controversies over industrialization, wage labor, women's rights, finance, immigration, slavery, territorial expansion, technological progress, and the whole question of the relation of individual and state, state and nation.

Whitman sent a copy of the 1855 *Leaves of Grass* to Ralph Waldo Emerson, whose response was immediate and generous: "I find it the most extraordinary piece of wit and wisdom that America has yet contributed." Spurred by Emerson's words of praise, Whitman published a second edition of *Leaves of Grass* with several new poems in 1856. While he was planning a third edition of *Leaves* as a kind of "New Bible" of democracy, Whitman had an unhappy love affair with a man. This tale of love and loss is the subject of a small sheaf of twelve poems, initially titled "Live Oak with Moss," which was later incorporated into the "Calamus" cluster in the 1860 *Leaves of Grass*. Whitman's homosexual love crisis along with the impending dissolution of the Union caused him to become increasingly doubtful about the future of America and his own future as the bard of democracy.

This doubt is evident in the 1860 edition of *Leaves of Grass*, particularly in the "Chants Democratic" and "Calamus" groupings, and in such individual poems as "Out of the Cradle Endlessly Rocking" and "As I Ebb'd with the Ocean of Life." In the poems of "Calamus," Whitman draws upon the language of democracy and phrenology to name his erotic feeling for men as both comradeship and "adhesiveness" (the phrenological term which Whitman defined as "the personal attachment of man to man"). The love poems of "Calamus" are paired with the procreation poems of "Children of Adam," which focus upon "amative" love, the phrenological term for the love between men and women. Although the press and the literary establishment immediately focused upon the "sex" poems of "Children of Adam" as Whitman's most provocative grouping, the love poems of "Calamus" were in fact his most radical sequence sexually and politically. Whitman infused the abstractions of democracy with the intensity of erotic passion, giving literature some of its first and most potent images of democratic comradeship; and by linking homoeroticism with a democratic breaking of bounds, he presents one of the most tender and moving accounts of homosexual love in Western literature.

For Whitman, as for the nation, the Civil War was a period of major crisis. Uncertain of the role of a national poet during a time of fratricidal war, Whitman published little during the war years. In 1862, when he went to the front in search of his brother George, he found the role he would play: he would become a kind of spiritual "wound-dresser" by visiting the sick and dying soldiers in the hospital wards of Washington. Like Lincoln's "Gettysburg Address," the poems of *Drum-Taps and Sequel* (1865–1866) and the prose of *Memoranda During the War* (1875–1876) were attempts to come to terms with the massive carnage of the war by placing its waste and apparent unreason within some larger providential design. In these volumes Whitman turns from romance to realism, vision to history, anticipating the naturalistic war writings of Stephen Crane, Ernest Hemingway, and Norman Mailer.

Whitman remained in Washington during and after the war, working first as a clerk in the Indian Bureau and then, after being dismissed in 1865 for moral turpitude by Secretary of the Interior James Harlan, in the Attorney General's office. For all Whitman's effort to (re)present the war as testing ground for democracy, the Civil War unleashed a hoard of psychic and socio-economic demons that would continue to haunt his dream of America in the postwar period.

In his incisive political essay *Democratic Vistas* (1871), which was initially composed as a response to Carlyle's attack on the "democratic rabble" in "Shooting Niagara," Whitman seeks to come to terms with the gilded monsters of post-Civil War America. Even before the worst scandals of the Grant administration were exposed,

he presents an image of America saturated in corruption and greed from the national to the local level. In "reconstructing, democratizing society" Whitman argues, the true "revolution" would be of the "interior life"; and in bringing about this democratic revolution, the poet would play the leading role by overhauling the "Culture theory" of the past and by providing the language, commonality, and myths by which America named itself. Like *Leaves of Grass, Democratic Vistas* works dialectically, as Whitman seeks to reconcile self and other, state and nation, North and South, country and city, labor and capital, money and soul. He arrives at no final synthesis of the values he seeks to juggle. Amid the modernizing, standardizing, and capitalizing whirl of America, where "with steam-engine speed" generations of humanity are turned out "like uniform iron castings," Whitman recognizes that the road to the future might be the road of the "fabled damned."

Whereas Whitman's war poems were merely tagged onto the end of the fourth edition of *Leaves,* which was published in 1867, in the 1871 *Leaves* these poems were incorporated into the main body of his work. By 1872, Whitman came to regard *Leaves of Grass* as essentially complete. In his 1872 "Preface" to "As a Strong Bird on Pinions Free," he announced his intention of turning away from his former emphasis on "a great composite *democratic individual,* male or female" toward an increased emphasis on "an aggregated, inseparable, unprecedented, vast, composite, electric *democratic nationality.*" His plan was cut short by a paralytic stroke which he suffered at the beginning of 1873. The seizure left him bedridden for several weeks and paralyzed for the rest of his life.

Whitman made a trip to Camden, New Jersey, a few days before his mother's death in May 1873, and never returned to Washington. He spent the remainder of his life in Camden, first at his brother George's house and finally, beginning in

1884, in his own home at 328 Mickle Street. Struggling with occasional spells of dizziness and a prematurely aging body, Whitman mustered enough strength to publish a dual volume of poetry and prose on the occasion of the American centennial in 1876. Invigorated by the visits to the New Jersey farm of Susan and George Stafford that he began making in 1876, by the economic recovery of the nation under the new political regime of Rutherford B. Hayes (1877–1881), and by the attention his work was beginning to receive in England and abroad, Whitman revised, reintegrated, and reordered all of his poems into the final 1881 edition of *Leaves of Grass.* In 1882, he published a prose companion to his poems titled *Specimen Days,* in which he refigures the events of his life and times as a narrative of personal, national, and cosmic restoration.

The poems that Whitman wrote in the last two decades of his life, such as "Passage to India" and "Prayer of Columbus," are characterized by a leap away from the physical landscape of America toward a more traditionally religious vision of God's providence and spiritual grace. Despite his apparent disillusionment with the material conditions of America, however, Whitman continued to name the possibility of an *other* America. Figuring himself in the image of a new-world Columbus, he continued to imagine the possibility of a democratic golden world which, like the dream of a passage to India and a world in round, might bloom in some future transformation of vision into history.

Betsy Erkkila
Northwestern University

PRIMARY WORKS

Malcolm Cowley, ed., *Leaves of Grass: The First (1855) Edition,* 1959; F. De Wolfe Miller, ed., *Drum-Taps and Sequel (1865–66): A Facsimile Reproduction,* 1959; Edwin H. Miller, ed., *The Correspondence (1842–1892),* 1961–69; Roy Harvey Pearce, ed., *Leaves of Grass: Facsimile of the 1860 Text,* 1961; *Memoranda During the War (1876): Facsimile,* 1962; Gay Wilson Allen and Sculley Bradley, eds., *The Collected Writings of Walt Whitman,* includes: Floyd Stovall, ed., *Prose Works (1892): Specimen Days, Collect, and Other Prose,* 1963; Thomas L. Brasher, ed., *The Early Poems and the Fiction,* 1963; Sculley Bradley and Harold Blodgett, eds., *Leaves of Grass: A Comprehensive Reader's Edition,* 1965; William White, ed., *Daybooks and Notebooks,* 1978; Sculley Bradley et al., eds., *Leaves of Grass: A Textual Variorum of the Printed Poems,* 1980; Edward F. Grier, ed., *Notebooks and Unpublished Prose Manuscripts,* 1984; Justin Kaplan, ed., *Whitman Poetry and Prose,* 1982; Edwin H. Miller, ed., *Selected Letters,* 1990; Herbert Bergman, Douglas A. Noverr, Edward J. Recchia, eds., *The Journalism/Walt Whitman,* 1998.

from Leaves of Grass

Preface to the 1855 Edition

America does not repel the past or what it has produced under its forms or amid other politics or the idea of castes or the old religions . . . . accepts the lesson with calmness . . . is not so impatient as has been supposed that the slough still sticks to opinions and manners and literature while the life which served its requirements has passed into the new life of the new forms . . . perceives that the corpse is slowly borne from the eating and sleeping rooms of the house . . . perceives that it waits a little while in the door . . . that it was fittest for its days . . . that its action has descended to the stalwart and wellshaped heir who approaches . . . and that he shall be fittest for his days.

The Americans of all nations at any time upon the earth have probably the fullest poetical nature. The United States themselves are essentially the greatest poem. In the history of the earth hitherto the largest and most stirring appear tame and orderly to their ampler largeness and stir. Here at last is something in the doings of man that corresponds with the broadcast doings of the day and night. Here is not merely a nation but a teeming nation of nations. Here is action untied from strings necessarily blind to particulars and details magnificently moving in vast masses. Here is the hospitality which forever indicates heroes. . . . Here are the roughs and beards and space and ruggedness and nonchalance that the soul loves. Here the performance disdaining the trivial unapproached in the tremendous audacity of its crowds and groupings and the push of its perspective spreads with crampless and flowing breadth and showers its prolific and splendid extravagance. One sees it must indeed own the riches of the summer and winter, and need never be bankrupt while corn grows from the ground or the orchards drop apples or the bays contain fish or men beget children upon women.

Other states indicate themselves in their deputies . . . . but the genius of the United States is not best or most in its executives or legislatures, nor in its ambassadors or authors or colleges or churches or parlors, nor even in its newspapers or inventors . . . but always most in the common people. Their manners speech dress friendships—the freshness and candor of their physiognomy—the picturesque looseness of their carriage . . . their deathless attachment to freedom—their aversion to anything indecorous or soft or mean—the practical acknowledgment of the citizens of one state by the citizens of all other states—the fierceness of their roused resentment—their curiosity and welcome of novelty—their self-esteem and wonderful sympathy—their susceptibility to a slight—the air they have of persons who never knew how it felt to stand in the presence of superiors—the fluency of their speech—their delight in music, the sure symptom of manly tenderness and native elegance of soul . . . their good temper and openhandedness—the terrible significance of their elections—the President's taking off his hat to them not they to him—these too are unrhymed poetry. It awaits the gigantic and generous treatment worthy of it.

The largeness of nature or the nation were monstrous without a corresponding largeness and generosity of the spirit of the citizen. Not nature nor swarming states nor streets and steamships nor prosperous business nor farms nor capital nor learning may suffice for the ideal of man . . . nor suffice the poet. No reminiscences may suffice either. A live nation can always cut a deep mark and can have the best authority the cheapest . . . namely from its own soul. This is the sum of the profitable uses of individuals or states and of present action and grandeur and of the subjects of poets.—As if it were necessary to trot back generation after generation to the eastern records! As if the beauty and sacredness of the demonstrable must fall behind that of the mythical! As if men do not make their mark out of any times! As if the opening of the western continent by discovery and what has transpired since in North and South America were less than the small theatre of the antique or the aimless sleepwalking of the middle ages! The pride of the United States leaves the wealth and finesse of the cities and all returns of commerce and agriculture and all the magnitude of geography or shows of exterior victory to enjoy the breed of fullsized men or one fullsized man unconquerable and simple.

The American poets are to enclose old and new for America is the race of races. Of them a bard is to be commensurate with a people. To him the other continents arrive as contributions . . . he gives them reception for their sake and his own sake. His spirit responds to his country's spirit . . . . he incarnates its geography and natural life and rivers and lakes. Mississippi with annual freshets and changing chutes, Missouri and Columbia and Ohio and Saint Lawrence with the falls and beautiful masculine Hudson, do not embouchure where they spend themselves more than they embouchure into him. The blue breadth over the inland sea of Virginia and Maryland and the sea off Massachusetts and Maine and over Manhattan bay and over Champlain and Erie and over Ontario and Huron and Michigan and Superior, and over the Texan and Mexican and Floridian and Cuban seas and over the seas off California and Oregon, is not tallied by the blue breadth of the waters below more than the breadth of above and below is tallied by him. When the long Atlantic coast stretches longer and the Pacific coast stretches longer he easily stretches with them north or south. He spans between them also from east to west and reflects what is between them. On him rise solid growths that offset the growths of pine and cedar and hemlock and liveoak and locust and chestnut and cypress and hickory and limetree and cottonwood and tuliptree and cactus and wildvine and tamarind and persimmon . . . . and tangles as tangled as any canebrake or swamp . . . . and forests coated with transparent ice and icicles hanging from the boughs and crackling in the wind . . . . and sides and peaks of mountains . . . . and pasturage sweet and free as savannah or upland or prairie . . . . with flights and songs and screams that answer those of the wildpigeon and highhold and orchard-oriole and coot and surf-duck and red-shouldered-hawk and fish-hawk and white-ibis and indian-hen and cat-owl and water-pheasant and qua-bird and pied-sheldrake and blackbird and mockingbird and buzzard and condor and night-heron and eagle. To him the hereditary countenance descends both mother's and father's. To him enter the essences of the real things and past and present events—of the enormous diversity of temperature and agriculture and mines—the tribes of red aborigines—the weather-beaten vessels entering new ports or making landings on rocky coasts—the first settlements north or south—the rapid stature and muscle—the haughty defiance of '76, and the war and peace and formation of the constitution . . . . the union always surrounded by blatherers and always calm and impregnable—the perpetual coming of immigrants—the wharfhem'd cities and superior marine—the unsurveyed interior—the loghouses and clearings and wild animals and hunters and trappers . . . . the free commerce—the fisheries and whaling and gold-digging—the endless gestation of new states—the convening of Congress every December, the members duly coming up from all climates and the uttermost parts . . . . the noble character of the young mechanics and of all free American workmen and workwomen . . . . the general ardor and friendliness and enterprise—the perfect equality of the female with the male . . . . the large amativeness—the fluid movement of the population—the factories and mercantile life and laborsaving machinery—the Yankee swap—the New-York firemen and the target excursion—the southern plantation life—the character of the northeast and of the northwest and southwest—slavery and the tremulous spreading of hands to protect it, and the stern opposition to it which shall never cease till it ceases or the speaking of tongues and the moving of lips cease. For such the expression of the American poet is to be transcendant and new. It is to be indirect and not direct or descriptive or epic. Its quality goes through these to much more. Let the age and wars of other nations be chanted and their eras and characters be illustrated and that finish the verse. Not so the great psalm of the republic. Here the theme is creative and has vista. Here comes one among the wellbeloved stonecutters and plans with decision and science and sees the solid and beautiful forms of the future where there are now no solid forms.

Of all nations the United States with veins full of poetical stuff most need poets and will doubtless have the greatest and use them the greatest. Their Presidents shall not be their common referee so much as their poets shall. Of all mankind the great poet is the equable man. Not in him but off from him things are grotesque or eccentric or fail of their sanity. Nothing out of its place is good and nothing in its place is bad. He bestows on every object or quality its fit proportions neither more nor less. He is the arbiter of the diverse and he is the key. He is the equalizer of his age and land . . . . he supplies what wants supplying and checks what wants checking. If peace is the routine out of him speaks the spirit of peace, large, rich, thrifty, building vast and populous cities, encouraging agriculture and the arts and commerce—lighting the study of man, the soul, immortality—federal, state or municipal government, marriage, health, freetrade, intertravel by land and sea . . . . nothing too close, nothing too far off . . . the stars not too far off. In war he is the most deadly force of the war. Who recruits him recruits horse and foot . . . he fetches parks of artillery the best that engineer ever knew. If the time becomes slothful and heavy he knows how to arouse it . . . he can make every word he speaks draw blood. Whatever stagnates in the flat of custom or obedience or legislation he never stagnates. Obedience does not master him, he masters it. High up out of reach he stands turning a concentrated light . . . he turns the pivot with his finger . . . he baffles the swiftest runners as he stands and easily overtakes and envelops them. The time straying toward infidelity and confections and persiflage he witholds by his steady faith . . . he spreads out his dishes . . . he offers the sweet firmfibred meat that grows men and women. His brain is the ultimate brain. He is no arguer . . . he is judgment. He judges not as the judge judges but as the sun falling around a helpless thing. As he sees the farthest he has the most faith. His thoughts are the hymns of the praise of things. In the talk on the soul and eternity and God off of his equal plane he is silent. He sees eternity less like a play with a prologue and denouement . . . . he sees eternity in men and women . . . he does not see men and women as dreams or dots. Faith is the antiseptic of the soul . . . it pervades the common people and preserves them . . . they never give up believing and expecting and trusting. There is that indescribable freshness and unconsciousness about an illiterate person that humbles and mocks the power of the noblest expressive genius. The poet sees for a certainty how one not a great artist may be just as sacred and perfect as the greatest artist. . . . . The power to destroy or remould is freely used by him but never the power of attack. What is past is past. If he does not expose superior models and prove himself by every step he takes he is not what is wanted. The presence of the greatest poet conquers . . . not parleying or struggling or any prepared attempts. Now he has passed that way see after him! there is not left any vestige of despair or misanthropy or cunning or exclusiveness or the ignominy of a nativity or color or delusion of hell or the necessity of hell . . . . . and no man thenceforward shall be degraded for ignorance or weakness or sin.

The greatest poet hardly knows pettiness or triviality. If he breathes into any thing that was before thought small it dilates with the grandeur and life of the universe. He is a seer . . . . he is individual . . . he is complete in himself . . . . the others are as good as he, only he sees it and they do not. He is not one of the chorus . . . . he does not stop for any regulation . . . he is the president of regulation. What the eyesight does to the rest he does to the rest. Who knows the curious mystery of the eyesight? The other senses corroborate themselves, but this is removed from any proof but its own and foreruns the identities of the spiritual world. A single glance of it mocks all the investigations of man and all the instruments and books of the earth and all reasoning. What is marvellous? what is unlikely? what is impossible or baseless or vague? after you have once just opened the space of a peachpit and given audience to far and near and to the sunset and had all things enter with electric swiftness softly and duly without confusion or jostling or jam.

The land and sea, the animals fishes and birds, the sky of heaven and the orbs, the forests mountains and rivers, are not small themes . . . but folks expect of the poet to indicate more than the beauty and dignity which always attach to dumb real objects . . . . they expect him to indicate the path between reality and their souls. Men and women perceive the beauty well enough . . probably as well as he. The passionate tenacity of hunters, woodmen, early risers, cultivators of gardens and orchards and fields, the love of healthy women for the manly form, seafaring persons, drivers of horses, the passion for light and the open air, all is an old varied sign of the unfailing perception of beauty and of a residence of the poetic in outdoor people. They can never be assisted by poets to perceive . . . some may but they never can. The poetic quality is not marshalled in rhyme or uniformity or abstract addresses to things nor in melancholy complaints or good precepts, but is the life of these and much else and is in the soul. The profit of rhyme is that it drops seeds of a sweeter and more luxuriant rhyme, and of uniformity that it conveys itself into its own roots in the ground out of sight. The rhyme and uniformity of perfect poems show the free growth of metrical laws and bud from them as unerringly and loosely as lilacs or roses on a bush, and take shapes as compact as the shapes of chestnuts and oranges and melons and pears, and shed the perfume impalpable to form. The fluency and ornaments of the finest poems or music or orations or recitations are not independent but dependent. All beauty comes from beautiful blood and a beautiful brain. If the greatnesses are in conjunction in a man or woman it is enough . . . . the fact will prevail through the universe . . . . but the gaggery and gilt of a million years will not prevail. Who troubles himself about his ornaments or fluency is lost. This is what you shall do: Love the earth and sun and the animals, despise riches, give alms to every one that asks, stand up for the stupid and crazy, devote your income and labor to others, hate tyrants, argue not concerning God, have patience and indulgence toward the people, take off your hat to nothing known or unknown or to any man or number of men, go freely with powerful uneducated persons and with the young and with the mothers of families, read these leaves in the open air every season of every year of your life, re-examine all you have been told at school or church or in any book, dismiss whatever insults you own soul, and your very flesh shall be a great poem and have the richest fluency not only in its words but in the silent lines of its lips and face and between the lashes of your eyes and in every motion and joint of your body . . . .
. . . . The poet shall not spend his time in unneeded work. He shall know that the ground is always ready ploughed and manured . . . . others may not know it but he

shall. He shall go directly to the creation. His trust shall master the trust of every-thing he touches . . . . and shall master all attachment.

The known universe has one complete lover and that is the greatest poet. He consumes an eternal passion and is indifferent which chance happens and which possible contingency of fortune or misfortune and persuades daily and hourly his delicious pay. What balks or breaks others is fuel for his burning progress to contact and amorous joy. Other proportions of the reception of pleasure dwindle to nothing to his proportions. All expected from heaven or from the highest he is rapport with in the sight of the daybreak or a scene of the winter woods or the presence of children playing or with his arm round the neck of a man or woman. His love above all love has leisure and expanse . . . . he leaves room ahead of himself. He is no irresolute or suspicious lover . . . he is sure . . . he scorns intervals. His experience and the showers and thrills are not for nothing. Nothing can jar him . . . . suffering and darkness cannot—death and fear cannot. To him complaint and jealousy and envy are corpses buried and rotten in the earth . . . . he saw them buried. The sea is not surer of the shore or the shore of the sea than he is of the fruition of his love and of all perfection and beauty.

The fruition of beauty is no chance of hit or miss . . . it is inevitable as life . . . . it is exact and plumb as gravitation. From the eyesight proceeds another eyesight and from the hearing proceeds another hearing and from the voice proceeds another voice eternally curious of the harmony of things with man. To these respond perfections not only in the committees that were supposed to stand for the rest but in the rest themselves just the same. These understand the law of perfection in masses and floods . . . that its finish is to each for itself and onward from itself . . . that it is profuse and impartial . . . that there is not a minute of the light or dark nor an acre of the earth or sea without it—nor any direction of the sky nor any trade or employment nor any turn of events. This is the reason that about the proper expression of beauty there is precision and balance . . . one part does not need to be thrust above another. The best singer is not the one who has the most lithe and powerful organ . . . the pleasure of poems is not in them that take the handsomest measure and similes and sound.

Without effort and without exposing in the least how it is done the greatest poet brings the spirit of any or all events and passions and scenes and persons some more and some less to bear on your individual character as you hear or read. To do this well is to compete with the laws that pursue and follow time. What is the purpose must surely be there and the clue of it must be there . . . . and the faintest indication is the indication of the best and then becomes the clearest indication. Past and present and future are not disjoined but joined. The greatest poet forms the consistence of what is to be from what has been and is. He drags the dead out of their coffins and stands them again on their feet . . . . he says to the past, Rise and walk before me that I may realize you. He learns the lesson . . . . he places himself where the future becomes present. The greatest poet does not only dazzle his rays over character and scenes and passions . . . he finally ascends and finishes all . . . he exhibits the pinnacles that no man can tell what they are for or what is beyond . . . . he glows a moment on the extremest verge. He is most wonderful in his last half-hidden smile or frown . . . by that flash of the moment of parting the one that sees it shall be encouraged or terrified afterward for many years. The greatest poet does not moralize or make applications of morals . . . he knows the soul. The soul has that measureless pride which consists in never acknowledging any lessons but its own. But it has sympathy as measureless as its pride and the one balances the other and neither can stretch too far while it stretches in company with the other. The inmost secrets of art sleep with the twain. The greatest poet has lain close betwixt both and they are vital in his style and thoughts.

The art of art, the glory of expression and the sunshine of the light of letters is simplicity. Nothing is better than simplicity . . . . nothing can make up for excess or for the lack of definiteness. To carry on the heave of impulse and pierce intellectual depths and give all subjects their articulations are powers neither common nor very uncommon. But to speak in literature with the perfect rectitude and insousiance of the movements of animals and the unimpeachableness of the sentiment of trees in the woods and grass by the roadside is the flawless triumph of art. If you have looked on him who has achieved it you have looked on one of the masters of the artists of all nations and times. You shall not contemplate the flight of the graygull over the bay or the mettlesome action of the blood horse or the tall leaning of sunflowers on their stalk or the appearance of the sun journeying through heaven or the appearance of the moon afterward with any more satisfaction than you shall contemplate him. The greatest poet has less a marked style and is more the channel of thoughts and things without increase or diminution, and is the free channel of himself. He swears to his art, I will not be meddlesome, I will not have in my writing any elegance or effect or originality to hang in the way between me and the rest like curtains. I will have nothing hang in the way, not the richest curtains. What I tell I tell for precisely what it is. Let who may exalt or startle or fascinate or soothe I will have purposes as health or heat or snow has and be as regardless of observation. What I experience or portray shall go from my composition without a shred of my composition. You shall stand by my side and look in the mirror with me.

The old red blood and stainless gentility of great poets will be proved by their unconstraint. A heroic person walks at his ease through and out of that custom or precedent or authority that suits him not. Of the traits of the brotherhood of writers savans[1] musicians inventors and artists nothing is finer than silent defiance advancing from new free forms. In the need of poems philosophy politics mechanism science behaviour, the craft of art, an appropriate native grand-opera, ship-craft, or any craft, he is greatest forever and forever who contributes the greatest original practical example. The cleanest expression is that which finds no sphere worthy of itself and makes one.

The messages of great poets to each man and women are, Come to us on equal terms, Only then can you understand us, We are no better than you, What we enclose you enclose, What we enjoy you may enjoy. Did you suppose there could be only one Supreme? We affirm there can be unnumbered Supremes, and that one does not countervail another any more than one eyesight countervails another . . and that men can be good or grand only of the consciousness of their supremacy within them. What do you think is the grandeur of storms and dismemberments and the deadliest battles and wrecks and the wildest fury of the elements and the power of the sea and the motion of nature and of the throes of human desires and dignity and hate and love? It is that something in the soul which says, Rage on, Whirl on, I tread

[1]Scientists.

master here and everywhere, Master of the spasms of the sky and of the shatter of the sea, Master of nature and passion and death, And of all terror and all pain.

The American bards shall be marked for generosity and affection and for encouraging competitors . . They shall be kosmos . . without monopoly or secrecy . . glad to pass any thing to any one . . hungry for equals night and day. They shall not be careful of riches and privilege . . . . they shall be riches and privilege . . . . they shall perceive who the most affluent man is. The most affluent man is he that confronts all the shows he sees by equivalents out of the stronger wealth of himself. The American bard shall delineate no class of persons nor one or two out of the strata of interests nor love most nor truth most nor the soul most nor the body most . . . . and not be for the eastern states more than the western or the northern states more than the southern.

Exact science and its practical movements are no checks on the greatest poet but always his encouragement and support. The outset and remembrance are there . . there the arms that lifted him first and brace him best . . . . there he returns after all his goings and comings. The sailor and traveler . . the anatomist chemist astronomer geologist phrenologist spiritualist mathematician historian and lexicographer are not poets, but they are the lawgivers of poets and their construction underlies the structure of every perfect poem. No matter what rises or is uttered they sent the seed of the conception of it . . . of them and by them stand the visible proofs of souls . . . . . always of their fatherstuff must be begotten the sinewy races of bards. If there shall be love and content between the father and the son and if the greatness of the son is the exuding of the greatness of the father there shall be love between the poet and the man of demonstrable science. In the beauty of poems are the tuft and final applause of science.

Great is the faith of the flush of knowledge and of the investigation of the depths of qualities and things. Cleaving and circling here swells the soul of the poet yet is president of itself always. The depths are fathomless and therefore calm. The innocence and nakedness are resumed . . . they are neither modest nor immodest. The whole theory of the special and supernatural and all that was twined with it or educed out of it departs as a dream. What has ever happened . . . . what happens and whatever may or shall happen, the vital laws enclose all . . . . they are sufficient for any case and for all cases . . . none to be hurried or retarded . . . . any miracle of affairs or persons inadmissible in the vast clear scheme where every motion and every spear of grass and the frames and spirits of men and women and all that concerns them are unspeakably perfect miracles all referring to all and each distinct and in its place. It is also not consistent with the reality of the soul to admit that there is anything in the known universe more divine than men and women.

Men and women and the earth and all upon it are simply to be taken as they are, and the investigation of their past and present and future shall be unintermitted and shall be done with perfect candor. Upon this basis philosophy speculates ever looking toward the poet, ever regarding the eternal tendencies of all toward happiness never inconsistent with what is clear to the senses and to the soul. For the eternal tendencies of all toward happiness make the only point of sane philosophy. Whatever comprehends less than that . . . whatever is less than the laws of light and of astronomical motion . . . or less than the laws that follow the thief the liar the glutton and the drunkard through this life and doubtless afterward . . . . . . or less than vast stretches of time or the slow formation of density or the patient upheaving of strata—is of no account. Whatever would put God in a poem or system of philosophy as contending against some being or influence is also of no account. Sanity and ensemble characterise the great master . . . spoilt in one principle all is spoilt. The great master has nothing to do with miracles. He sees health for himself in being one of the mass . . . . he sees the hiatus in singular eminence. To the perfect shape comes common ground. To be under the general law is great for that is to correspond with it. The master knows that he is unspeakably great and that all are unspeakably great . . . . that nothing for instance is greater than to conceive children and bring them up well . . . that to be is just as great as to perceive or tell.

In the make of the great masters the idea of political liberty is indispensible. Liberty takes the adherence of heroes wherever men and women exist . . . . but never takes any adherence or welcome from the rest more than from poets. They are the voice and exposition of liberty. They out of ages are worthy the grand idea . . . . to them it is confided and they must sustain it. Nothing has precedence of it and nothing can warp or degrade it. The attitude of great poets is to cheer up slaves and horrify despots. The turn of their necks, the sound of their feet, the motions of their wrists, are full of hazard to the one and hope to the other. Come nigh them awhile and though they neither speak or advise you shall learn the faithful American lesson. Liberty is poorly served by men whose good intent is quelled from one failure or two failures or any number of failures, or from the casual indifference or ingratitude of the people, or from the sharp show of the tushes of power, or the bringing to bear soldiers and cannon or any penal statutes. Liberty relies upon itself, invites no one, promises nothing, sits in calmness and light, is positive and composed, and knows no discouragement. The battle rages with many a loud alarm and frequent advance and retreat . . . . the enemy triumphs . . . . the prison, the handcuffs, the iron necklace and anklet, the scaffold, garrote and leadballs do their work . . . . the cause is asleep . . . . the strong throats are choked with their own blood . . . . the young men drop their eyelashes toward the ground when they pass each other . . . . and is liberty gone out of that place? No never. When liberty goes it is not the first to go nor the second or third to go . . it waits for all the rest to go . . it is the last. . . When the memories of the old martyrs are faded utterly away . . . . when the large names of patriots are laughed at in the public halls from the lips of the orators . . . . when the boys are no more christened after the same but christened after tyrants and traitors instead . . . . when the laws of the free are grudgingly permitted and laws for informers and blood-money are sweet to the taste of the people . . . . when I and you walk abroad upon the earth stung with compassion at the sight of numberless brothers answering our equal friendship and calling no man master—and when we are elated with noble joy at the sight of slaves . . . . when the soul retires in the cool communion of the night and surveys its experience and has much extasy over the word and deed that put back a helpless innocent person into the gripe of the gripers or into any cruel inferiority . . . . when those in all parts of these states who could easier realize the true American character but do not yet—when the swarms of cringers, suckers, dough-faces, lice of politics, planners of sly involutions for their own preferment to city offices or state legislatures or the judiciary or congress or the presidency, obtain a response of love and natural deference from the people whether they get the offices or no . . . . when it is better to be a bound booby and rogue in office at a high salary than the poorest free mechanic or farmer with his hat unmoved from his head and firm eyes and a candid and generous heart . . . . and when servility by town or state or the federal government or any oppression on a large scale or small scale can be tried on without its own punishment following duly after in exact proportion against the smallest chance of escape . . . . or rather when all life and all the souls of men and women are discharged from that part of the earth.

As the attributes of the poets of the kosmos concentre in the real body and soul and in the pleasure of things they possess the superiority of genuineness over all fiction and romance. As they emit themselves facts are showered over with light . . . . the daylight is lit with more volatile light . . . . also the deep between the setting and rising sun goes deeper many fold. Each precise object or condition or combination or process exhibits a beauty . . . . the multiplication table its—old age its—the carpenter's trade its—the grand-opera its . . . . the hugehulled clean-shaped New-York clipper at sea under steam or full sail gleams with unmatched beauty . . . . the American circles and large harmonies of government gleam with theirs . . . . and the commonest definite intentions and actions with theirs. The poets of the kosmos advance through all interpositions and coverings and turmoils and stratagems to first principles. They are of use . . . . they dissolve poverty from its need and riches from its conceit. You large proprietor they say shall not realize or perceive more than any one else. The owner of the library is not he who holds a legal title to it having bought and paid for it. Any one and every one is owner of the library who can read the same through all the varieties of tongues and subjects and styles, and in whom they enter with ease and take residence and force toward paternity and maternity, and make supple and powerful and rich and large. . . . . These American states strong and healthy and accomplished shall receive no pleasure from violations of natural models and must not permit them. In paintings or mouldings or carvings in mineral or wood, or in the illustrations of books or newspapers, or in any comic or tragic prints, or in the patterns of woven stuffs or any thing to beautify rooms or furniture or costumes, or to put upon cornices or monuments or on the prows or sterns of ships, or to put anywhere before the human eye indoors or out, that which distorts honest shapes or which creates unearthly beings or places or contingencies is a nuisance and revolt. Of the human form especially it is so great it must never be made ridiculous. Of ornaments to a work nothing outre[2] can be allowed . . but those ornaments can be allowed that conform to the perfect facts of the open air and that flow out of the nature of the work and come irrepressibly from it and are necessary to the completion of the work. Most works are most beautiful without ornament. . . Exaggerations will be revenged in human physiology. Clean and vigorous children are jetted and conceived only in those communities where the models of natural forms are public every day. . . . . . Great genius and the people of these states must never be demeaned to romances. As soon as histories are properly told there is no more need of romances.

The great poets are also to be known by the absence in them of tricks and by the justification of perfect personal candor. Then folks echo a new cheap joy and a divine voice leaping from their brains: How beautiful is candor! All faults may be forgiven of him who has perfect candor. Henceforth let no man of us lie, for we have

---

[2]Excessive, extravagant. An example of Whitman's many "borrowings" from the French language.

seen that openness wins the inner and outer world and that there is no single exception, and that never since our earth gathered itself in a mass have deceit or subterfuge or prevarication attracted its smallest particle or the faintest tinge of a shade—and that through the enveloping wealth and rank of a state or the whole republic of states a sneak or sly person shall be discovered and despised . . . . and that the soul has never been once fooled and never can be fooled . . . . and thrift without the loving nod of the soul is only a fœtid puff . . . . and there never grew up in any of the continents of the globe nor upon any planet or satellite or star, nor upon the asteroids, nor in any part of ethereal space, nor in the midst of density, nor under the fluid wet of the sea, nor in that condition which precedes the birth of babes, nor at any time during the changes of life, nor in that condition that follows what we term death, nor in any stretch of abeyance or action afterward of vitality, nor in any process of formation or reformation anywhere, a being whose instinct hated the truth.

Extreme caution or prudence, the soundest organic health, large hope and comparison and fondness for women and children, large alimentiveness and destructiveness and causality, with a perfect sense of the oneness of nature and the propriety of the same spirit applied to human affairs . . these are called up of the float of the brain of the world to be parts of the greatest poet from his birth out of his mother's womb and from her birth out of her mother's. Caution seldom goes far enough. It has been thought that the prudent citizen was the citizen who applied himself to solid gains and did well for himself and his family and completed a lawful life without debt or crime. The greatest poet sees and admist these economies as he sees the economies of food and sleep, but has higher notions of prudcence than to think he gives much when he gives a few slight attentions at the latch of the gate. The premises of the prudence of life are not the hospitality of it or the ripeness and harvest of it. Beyond the independence of a little sum laid aside for burial-money, and of a few clap-boards around and shingles overhead on a lot of American soil owned, and the easy dollars that supply the year's plain clothing and meals, the melancholy prudence of the abandonment of such a great being as a man is to the toss and pallor of years of money-making with all their scorching days and icy nights and all their stifling deceits and underhanded dodgings, or infinitessimals of parlors, or shameless stuffing while others starve . . and all the loss of the bloom and odor of the earth and of the flowers and atmosphere and of the sea and of the true taste of the women and men you pass or have to do with in youth or middle age, and the issuing sickness and desperate revolt at the close of a life without elevation or naivete, and the ghastly chatter of a death without serenity or majesty, is the great fraud upon modern civilization and forethought, blotching the surface and system which civilization undeniably drafts, and moistening with tears the immense features it spreads and spreads with such velocity before the reached kisses of the soul. . . Still the right explanation remains to be made about prudence. The prudence of the mere wealth and respectability of the most esteemed life appears too faint for the eye to observe at all when little and large alike drop quietly aside at the thought of the prudence suitable for immortality. What is wisdom that fills the thinness of a year or seventy or eighty years to wisdom spaced out by ages and coming back at a certain time with strong reinforcements and rich presents and the clear faces of wedding-guests as far as you can look in every direction running gaily toward you? Only the soul is of itself . . . . all else has reference to what ensues. All that a person does or thinks is of consequence. Not a move can a man or woman make that affects him or her in a day or a month or any part of the direct lifetime or the hour of death but the same affects him or her onward afterward through the indirect lifetime. The indirect is always as great and real as the direct. The spirit receives from the body just as much as it gives to the body. Not one name of word or deed . . not of venereal sores or discolorations . . not the privacy of the onanist . . not of the putrid veins of gluttons or rumdrinkers . . . not peculation or cunning or betrayal or murder . . no serpentine poision of those that seduce women . . not the foolish yielding of women . . not prostitution . . not of any depravity of young men . . not of the attainment of gain by discreditable means . . not any nastiness of appetite . . not any harshness of officers to men or judges to prisoners or fathers to sons or sons to fathers or of husbands to wives or bosses to their boys . . not of greedy looks or malignant wishes . . . nor any of the wiles practised by people upon themselves . . . ever is or ever can be stamped on the programme but it is duly realized and returned, and that returned in further performances . . . and they returned again. Nor can the push of charity or personal force ever be any thing else than the profoundest reason, whether it bring arguments to hand or no. No specification is necessary . . to add or subtract or divide is in vain. Little or big, learned or unlearned, white or black, legal or illegal, sick or well, from the first inspiration down the windpipe to the last expiration out of it, all that a male or female does that is vigorous and benevolent and clean is so much sure profit to him or her in the unshakable order of the universe and through the whole scope of it forever. If the savage or felon is wise it is well . . . . if the greatest poet or savan is wise it is simply the same . . if the President or chief justice is wise it is the same . . . if the young mechanic or farmer is wise it is no more or less . . if the prositute is wise it is no more nor less. The interest will come round . . all will come round. All the best actions of war and peace . . . all help given to relatives and strangers and the poor and old and sorrowful and young children and widows and the sick, and to all shunned persons . . all furtherance of fugitives and of the escape of slaves . . all the self-denial that stood steady and aloof on wrecks and saw others take the seats of the boats . . . all offering of substance or life for the good old cause, or for a friend's sake or opinion's sake . . . all pains of enthusiasts scoffed at by their neighbors . . all the vast sweet love and precious suffering of mothers . . . all honest men baffled in strifes recorded or unrecorded . . . . all the grandeur and good of the few ancient nations whose fragments of annals we inherit . . and all the good of the hundreds of far mightier and more ancient nations unknown to us by name or date or location . . . . all that was ever manfully begun, whether it succeeded or no . . . . all that has at any time been well suggested out of the divine heart of man or by the divinity of his mouth or by the shaping of his great hands . . and all that is well thought or done this day on any part of the surface of the globe . . or on any of the wandering stars or fixed stars by those there as we are here . . or that is henceforth to be well thought or done by you whoever you are, or by any one—these singly and wholly inured at their time and inure now and will inure always to the identities from which they sprung or shall spring. . . Did you guess any of them lived only its moment? The world does not so exist . . no parts palpable or impalpable so exist . . . no result exists now without being from its long antecedent result, and that from its antecdent, and so backward without the farthest mentionable spot coming a bit nearer the beginning than any other spot. . . . . Whatever satisfies the soul is truth. The prudence of the greatest poet answers at last the craving and glut of the soul, is not contemptuous of less ways of prudence if they conform to its ways, puts off nothing, permits no let-up for its own case or any case, has no particular sabbath or judgment-day, divides not the living from the dead or the righteous from the unrighteous, is satisfied with the present, matches every thought or act by its correlative, knows no possible forgiveness or deputed atonement . . knows that the young man who composedly periled his life and lost it has done exceeding well for himself, while the man who has not periled his life and retains it to old age in riches and ease has perhaps achieved nothing for himself worth mentioning . . and that only that person has no great prudence to learn who has learnt to prefer real longlived things, and favors body and soul the same, and perceives the indirect assuredly following the direct, and what evil or good he does leaping onward and waiting to meet him again—and who in his spirit in any emergency whatever neither hurries or avoids death.

The direct trial of him who would be the greatest poet is today. If he does not flood himself with the immediate age as with vast oceanic tides . . . . . and if he does not attract his own land body and soul to himself and hang on its neck with incomparable love and plunge his semitic[3] muscle into its merits and demerits . . . and if he be not himself the age transfigured . . . . and if to him is not opened the eternity which gives similitude to all periods and locations and processes and animate and inanimate forms, and which is the bond of time, and rises up from its inconceivable vagueness and infiniteness in the swimming shape of today, and is held by the ductile anchors of life, and makes the present spot the passage from what was to what shall be, and commits itself to the representation of this wave of an hour and this one of the sixty beautiful children of the wave—let him merge in the general run and wait his development. . . . . Still the final test of poems or any character or work remains. The prescient poet projects himself centuries ahead and judges performer or performance after the changes of time. Does it live through them? Does it still hold on untired? Will the same style and the direction of genius to similar points be satisfactory now? Has no new discovery in science or arrival at superior planes of thought and judgment and behaviour fixed him or his so that either can be looked down upon? Have the marches of tens and hundreds and thousands of years made willing detours to the right hand and the left hand for his sake? Is he beloved long and long after he is buried? Does the young man think often of him? and the young woman think often of him? and do the middleaged and the old think of him?

A great poem is for ages and ages in common and for all degrees and complexions and all departments and sects and for a woman as much as a man and a man as much as a woman. A great poem is no finish to a man or woman but rather a beginning. Has any one fancied he could sit at last under some due authority and rest satisfied with explanations and realize and be content and full? To no such terminus does the greatest poet bring . . . he brings neither cessation or sheltered fatness and ease. The touch of him tells in action. Whom he takes he takes with firm sure grasp into live regions previously unattained . . . . thenceforward is no rest . . . . they see the space and ineffable sheen that turn the old spots and lights into dead vacuums. The companion of him beholds the birth and progress of stars and learns one of the meanings. Now there shall be a man cohered out of tumult and chaos . . . . the elder encourages the younger and shows him how . . . they two shall launch off fearlessly

[3]Whitman's own rather awkward coinage, suggesting the sexual organ through which semen passes.

together till the new world fits an orbit for itself and looks unabashed on the lesser orbits of the stars and sweeps through the ceaseless rings and shall never be quiet again.

There will soon be no more priests. Their work is done. They may wait awhile .. perhaps a generation or two .. dropping off by degrees. A superior breed shall take their place . . . . the gangs of kosmos and prophets en masse shall take their place. A new order shall arise and they shall be the priests of man, and every man shall be his own priest. The churches built under their umbrage shall be the churches of men and women. Through the divinity of themselves shall the kosmos and the new breed of poets be interpreters of men and women and of all events and things. They shall find their inspiration in real objects today, symptoms of the past and future . . . . They shall not deign to defend immortality or God or the perfection of things or liberty or the exquisite beauty and reality of the soul. They shall arise in America and be responded to from the remainder of the earth.

The English language befriends the grand American expression . . . . it is brawny enough and limber and full enough. On the tough stock of a race who through all change of circumstance was never without the idea of political liberty, which is the animus of all liberty, it has attracted the terms of daintier and gayer and subtler and more elegant tongues. It is the powerful language of resistance . . . it is the dialect of common sense. It is the speech of the proud and melancholy races and of all who aspire. It is the chosen tongue to express growth faith self-esteem freedom justice equality friendliness amplitude prudence decision and courage. It is the medium that shall well nigh express the inexpressible.

No great literature nor any like style of behaviour or oratory or social intercourse or household arrangements or public institutions or the treatment by bosses of employed people, nor executive detail or detail of the army or navy, nor spirit of legislation or courts or police or tuition or architecture or songs or amusements or the costumes of young men, can long elude the jealous and passionate instinct of American standards. Whether or no the sign appears from the mouths of the people, it throbs a live interrogation in every freeman's and freewoman's heart after that which passes by or this built to remain. Is it uniform with my country? Are its disposals without ignominious distinctions? Is it for the evergrowing communes of brothers and lovers, large, well-united, proud beyond the old models, generous beyond all models? Is it something grown fresh out of the fields or drawn from the sea for use to me today here? I know that what answers for me an American must answer for any individual or nation that serves for a part of my materials. Does this answer? or is it without reference to universal needs? or sprung of the needs of the less developed society of special ranks? or old needs of pleasure overlaid by modern science and forms? Does this acknowledge liberty with audible and absolute acknowledgement, and set slavery at nought for life and death? Will it help breed one goodshaped and wellhung man, and a woman to be his perfect and independent mate? Does it improve manners? Is it for the nursing of the young of the republic? Does it solve readily with the sweet milk of the nipples of the breasts of the mother of many children? Has it too the old ever-fresh forbearance and impartiality? Does it look with the same love on the last born and on those hardening toward stature, and on the errant, and on those who disdain all strength of assault outside of their own?

The poems distilled from other poems will probably pass away. The coward will surely pass away. The expectation of the vital and great can only be satisfied by the demeanor of the vital and great. The swarms of the polished deprecating and reflectors and the polite float off and leave no remembrance. America prepares with composure and goodwill for the visitors that have sent word. It is not intellect that is to be their warrant and welcome. The talented, the artist, the ingenious, the editor, the statesman, the erudite . . . they are not unappreciated . . . they fall in their place and do their work. The soul of the nation also does its work. No disguise can pass on it . . . no disguise can conceal from it. It rejects none, it permits all. Only toward as good as itself and toward the like of itself will it advance half-way. An individual is as superb as a nation when he has the qualities which make a superb nation. The soul of the largest and wealthiest and proudest nation may well go half-way to meet that of its poets. The signs are effectual. There is no fear of mistake. If the one is true the other is true. The proof of a poet is that his country absorbs him as affectionately as he has absorbed it.

Song of Myself[1]

[1]   I celebrate myself,
            And what I assume you shall assume,
            For every atom belonging to me as good belongs to you.

            I loafe and invite my soul,
5   I lean and loafe at my ease . . . . observing a spear of summer
              grass.

[2]   Houses and rooms are full of perfumes . . . . the shelves are
              crowded with perfumes,
            I breathe the fragrance myself, and know it and like it,
            The distillation would intoxicate me also, but I shall not let it.

            The atmosphere is not a perfume . . . . it has no taste of the
              distillation . . . . it is odorless,

[1]"Song of Myself" was the first of the twelve untitled poems that followed the Preface in the first edition of *Leaves of Grass* (1855). In the 1856 *Leaves* it was titled "Poem of Walt Whitman, An American." It was not until the final edition of *Leaves of Grass* in 1881 that the poem was titled "Song of Myself." We have used the 1855 versions of "Song of Myself," "The Sleepers," and "There Was a Child Went Forth" because in later editions of the poems, Whitman toned down some of the more radical stylistic, linguistic, and thematic features of the original edition of *Leaves of Grass*. For the convenience of readers familiar with the later version of "Song of Myself," which is divided into fifty-two sections, we have provided the section numbers in marginal brackets at the point at which each section begins in the 1881 edition. The line numbers will not, of course, correspond to those of later versions of the poem, since Whitman added and, less frequently, deleted lines from the text.

10 It is for my mouth forever . . . . I am in love with it,
    I will go to the bank by the wood and become undisguised and
        naked,
    I am mad for it to be in contact with me.

    The smoke of my own breath,
    Echos, ripples, and buzzed whispers . . . . loveroot, silkthread,
        crotch and vine,
15 My respiration and inspiration . . . . the beating of my heart . . . .
        the passing of blood and air through my lungs,
    The sniff of green leaves and dry leaves, and of the shore and
        darkcolored sea-rocks, and of hay in the barn,
    The sound of the belched words of my voice . . . . words loosed
        to the eddies of the wind,
    A few light kisses . . . . a few embraces . . . . a reaching around of
        arms,
    The play of shine and shade on the trees as the supple boughs
        wag,
20 The delight alone or in the rush of the streets, or along the fields
        and hillsides,
    The feeling of health . . . . the full-noon trill . . . . the song of me
        rising from bed and meeting the sun.

    Have you reckoned a thousand acres much? Have you reckoned
        the earth much?
    Have you practiced so long to learn to read?
    Have you felt so proud to get at the meaning of poems?

25 Stop this day and night with me and you shall possess the origin
        of all poems,
    You shall possess the good of the earth and sun . . . . there are
        millions of suns left,
    You shall no longer take things at second or third hand . . . . nor
        look through the eyes of the dead . . . . nor feed on the
        spectres in books,
    You shall not look through my eyes either, nor take things from
        me,
    You shall listen to all sides and filter them from yourself.

[3]   30 I have heard what the talkers were talking . . . . the talk of the
        beginning and the end,
    But I do not talk of the beginning or the end.

    There was never any more inception than there is now,
    Nor any more youth or age than there is now;
    And will never be any more perfection than there is now,
35 Nor any more heaven or hell than there is now.

Urge and urge and urge,
Always the procreant urge of the world.

Out of the dimness opposite equals advance . . . . Always
    substance and increase,
Always a knit of identity . . . . always distinction . . . . always a
    breed of life.
40 To elaborate is no avail . . . . Learned and unlearned feel that it is
    so.

Sure as the most certain sure . . . . plumb in the uprights, well
    entretied, braced in the beams,
Stout as a horse, affectionate, haughty, electrical,
I and this mystery here we stand.

Clear and sweet is my soul . . . . and clear and sweet is all that is
    not my soul.

45 Lack one lacks both . . . . and the unseen is proved by the seen,
Till that becomes unseen and receives proof in its turn.

Showing the best and dividing it from the worst, age vexes age,
Knowing the perfect fitness and equanimity of things, while they
    discuss I am silent, and go bathe and admire myself.

Welcome is every organ and attribute of me, and of any man
    hearty and clean,
50 Not an inch nor a particle of an inch is vile, and none shall be less
    familiar than the rest.

I am satisfied . . . . I see, dance, laugh, sing;
As God comes a loving bedfellow and sleeps at my side all night
    and close on the peep of the day,
And leaves for me baskets covered with white towels bulging the
    house with their plenty,
Shall I postpone my acceptation and realization and scream at my
    eyes,
55 That they turn from gazing after and down the road,
And forthwith cipher and show me to a cent,
Exactly the contents of one, and exactly the contents of two, and
    which is ahead?

[4]   Trippers and askers surround me,
People I meet . . . . . the effect upon me of my early life . . . . of
    the ward and city I live in . . . . of the nation,
60 The latest news . . . . discoveries, inventions, societies . . . .
    authors old and new,

My dinner, dress, associates, looks, business, compliments, dues,
The real or fancied indifference of some man or woman I love,
The sickness of one of my folks—or of myself . . . . or illdoing
    . . . . or loss or lack of money . . . . or depressions or
    exaltations,
They come to me days and nights and go from me again,
65 But they are not the Me myself.

Apart from the pulling and hauling stands what I am,
Stands amused, complacent, compassionating, idle, unitary,
Looks down, is erect, bends an arm on an impalpable certain rest,
Looks with its sidecurved head curious what will come next,
70 Both in and out of the game, and watching and wondering at it.

Backward I see in my own days where I sweated through fog with
    linguists and contenders,
I have no mockings or arguments . . . . I witness and wait.

[5]   I believe in you my soul . . . . the other I am must not abase itself
    to you,
And you must not be abased to the other.

75 Loafe with me on the grass . . . . loose the stop from your throat,
Not words, not music or rhyme I want . . . . not custom or
    lecture, not even the best,
Only the lull I like, the hum of your valved voice.

I mind how we lay in June, such a transparent summer morning;
You settled your head athwart my hips and gently turned over
    upon me,
80 And parted the shirt from my bosom-bone, and plunged your
    tongue to my barestript heart,
And reached till you felt my beard, and reached till you held my
    feet.

Swiftly arose and spread around me the peace and joy and
    knowledge that pass all the art and argument of the earth;
And I know that the hand of God is the elderhand of my own,
And I know that the spirit of God is the eldest brother of my
    own,
85 And that all the men ever born are also my brothers . . . . and the
    women my sisters and lovers,
And that a kelson[2] of the creation is love;
And limitless are leaves stiff or drooping in the fields,

---

[2]A structural unit that connects or reinforces,
like the keelson that braces the keel of a ship.

And brown ants in the little wells beneath them,
And mossy scabs of the wormfence, and heaped stones, and elder
  and mullen and pokeweed.

[6]   90 A child said, What is the grass? fetching it to me with full hands;

How could I answer the child? . . . . I do not know what it is any
  more than he.

I guess it must be the flag of my disposition, out of hopeful green
  stuff woven.

Or I guess it is the handkerchief of the Lord,
A scented gift and remembrancer designedly dropped,
95 Bearing the owner's name someway in the corners, that we may see
  and remark, and say Whose?

Or I guess the grass is itself a child . . . . the produced babe of
  the vegetation.

Or I guess it is a uniform hieroglyphic,
And it means, Sprouting alike in broad zones and narrow zones,
Growing among black folks as among white,
100 Kanuck, Tuckahoe, Congressman, Cuff,[3] I give them the same, I
  receive them the same.

And now it seems to me the beautiful uncut hair of graves.

Tenderly will I use you curling grass,
It may be you transpire from the breasts of young men,
It may be if I had known them I would have loved them;
105 It may be you are from old people and from women, and from
  offspring taken soon out of their mothers' laps,
And here you are the mothers' laps.

This grass is very dark to be from the white heads of old mothers,
Darker than the colorless beards of old men,
Dark to come from under the faint red roofs of mouths.

110 O I perceive after all so many uttering tongues!
And I perceive they do not come from the roofs of mouths for
  nothing.

I wish I could translate the hints about the dead young men and
  women,

---

[3]Kanuck, a French Canadian; Tuckahoe, a Vir-
ginian; Cuff, a black person.

And the hints about old men and mothers, and the offspring taken
    soon out of their laps.

What do you think has become of the young and old men?
115 And what do you think has become of the women and children?

They are alive and well somewhere;
The smallest sprout shows there is really no death,
And if ever there was it led forward life, and does not wait at the
    end to arrest it,
And ceased the moment life appeared.

120 All goes onward and outward . . . . and nothing collapses,
And to die is different from what any one supposed, and luckier.

[7]   Has any one supposed it lucky to be born?
I hasten to inform him or her it is just as lucky to die, and I know
    it.

I pass death with the dying, and birth with the new-washed babe
    . . . . and am not contained between my hat and boots,
125 And peruse manifold objects, no two alike, and every one good,
The earth good, and the stars good, and their adjuncts all good.
I am not an earth nor an adjunct of an earth,
I am the mate and companion of people, all just as immortal and
    fathomless as myself;
They do not know how immortal, but I know.

130 Every kind for itself and its own . . . . for me mine male and
    female,
For me all that have been boys and that love women,
For me the man that is proud and feels how it stings to be
    slighted,
For me the sweetheart and the old maid . . . . for me mothers and
    the mothers of mothers,
For me lips that have smiled, eyes that have shed tears,
135 For me children and the begetters of children.

Who need be afraid of the merge?
Undrape . . . . you are not guilty to me, nor stale nor discarded,
I see through the broadcloth and gingham whether or no,
And am around, tenacious, acquisitive, tireless . . . . and can never
    be shaken away.

[8]   140 The little one sleeps in its cradle,
I lift the gauze and look a long time, and silently brush away flies
    with my hand.

The youngster and the redfaced girl turn aside up the bushy hill,
I peeringly view them from the top.

The suicide sprawls on the bloody floor of the bedroom.
145 It is so . . . . I witnessed the corpse . . . . there the pistol had
    fallen.

The blab of the pave . . . . the tires of carts and sluff of bootsoles
    and talk of the promenaders,
The heavy omnibus, the driver with his interrogating thumb, the
    clank of the shod horses on the granite floor,
The carnival of sleighs, the clinking and shouted jokes and pelts of
    snowballs;
The hurrahs for popular favorites . . . . the fury of roused mobs,
150 The flap of the curtained litter—the sick man inside, borne to the
    hospital,
The meeting of enemies, the sudden oath, the blows and fall,
The excited crowd—the policeman with his star quickly working
    his passage to the centre of the crowd;
The impassive stones that receive and return so many echoes,
The souls moving along . . . . are they invisible while the least
    atom of the stones is visible?
155 What groans of overfed or half-starved who fall on the flags[4]
    sunstruck or in fits,
What exclamations of women taken suddenly, who hurry home
    and give birth to babes,
What living and buried speech is always vibrating here . . . . what
    howls restrained by decorum,
Arrests of criminals, slights, adulterous offers made, acceptances,
    rejections with convex lips,
I mind them or the resonance of them . . . . I come again and
    again.

[9]   160 The big doors of the country-barn stand open and ready,
The dried grass of the harvest-time loads the slow-drawn
    wagon,
The clear light plays on the brown gray and green intertinged,
The armfuls are packed to the sagging mow:
I am there . . . . I help . . . . I came stretched atop of the load,
165 I felt its soft jolts . . . . one leg reclined on the other,
I jump from the crossbeams, and seize the clover and timothy,
And roll head over heels, and tangle my hair full of wisps.

[10]   Alone far in the wilds and mountains I hunt,
Wandering amazed at my own lightness and glee,

---

[4]Slabs of flagstone used for paving.

170 In the late afternoon choosing a safe spot to pass the night,
    Kindling a fire and broiling the freshkilled game,
    Soundly falling asleep on the gathered leaves, my dog and gun by
        my side.

    The Yankee clipper is under her three skysails . . . . she cuts the
        sparkle and scud,
    My eyes settle the land . . . . I bend at her prow or shout joyously
        from the deck.

175 The boatmen and clamdiggers arose early and stopped for me,
    I tucked my trowser-ends in my boots and went and had a good
        time,
    You should have been with us that day round the chowder-kettle.

    I saw the marriage of the trapper in the open air in the farwest
        . . . . the bride was a red girl,
    Her father and his friends sat near by crosslegged and dumbly
        smoking . . . . they had moccasins to their feet and large thick
        blankets hanging from their shoulders;
180 On a bank lounged the trapper . . . . he was dressed mostly in
        skins . . . . his luxuriant beard and curls protected his neck,
    One hand rested on his rifle . . . . the other hand held firmly the
        wrist of the red girl,
    She had long eyelashes . . . . her head was bare . . . . her coarse
        straight locks descended upon her voluptuous limbs and
        reached to her feet.

    The runaway slave[5] came to my house and stopped outside,
    I heard his motions crackling the twigs of the woodpile,
185 Through the swung half-door of the kitchen I saw him limpsey and
        weak,
    And went where he sat on a log, and led him in and assured him,
    And brought water and filled a tub for his sweated body and
        bruised feet,
    And gave him a room that entered from my own, and gave him
        some coarse clean clothes,
    And remember perfectly well his revolving eyes and his
        awkwardness,
190 And remember putting plasters on the galls of his neck and ankles;
    He staid with me a week before he was recuperated and passed north,
    I had him sit next me at table . . . . my firelock leaned in the
        corner.

---

[5]A new and more rigorous Fugitive Slave Act, which required that inhabitants of the free states assist in the capture and return of runaway slaves, was adopted as part of the politically controversial Compromise of 1850.

[11]   Twenty-eight young men bathe by the shore,
                Twenty-eight young men, and all so friendly,
195 Twenty-eight years of womanly life, and all so lonesome.

                She owns the fine house by the rise of the bank,
                She hides handsome and richly drest aft the blinds of the window.

                Which of the young men does she like the best?
                Ah the homeliest of them is beautiful to her.

200 Where are you off to, lady? for I see you,
                You splash in the water there, yet stay stock still in your room.

                Dancing and laughing along the beach came the twenty-ninth
                    bather,
                The rest did not see her, but she saw them and loved them.

                The beards of the young men glistened with wet, it ran from their
                    long hair,
205 Little streams passed all over their bodies.

                An unseen hand also passed over their bodies,
                It descended tremblingly from their temples and ribs.

                The young men float on their backs, their white bellies swell to the
                    sun . . . . they do not ask who seizes fast to them,
                They do not know who puffs and declines with pendant and
                    bending arch,
210 They do not think whom they souse with spray.

[12]   The butcher-boy puts off his killing-clothes, or sharpens his knife
                    at the stall in the market,
                I loiter enjoying his repartee and his shuffle and breakdown.[6]
                Blacksmiths with grimed and hairy chests environ the anvil,
                Each has his main-sledge . . . . they are all out . . . . there is a
                    great heat in the fire.

215 From the cinder-strewed threshold I follow their movements,
                The lithe sheer of their waists plays even with their massive arms,
                Overhand the hammers roll—overhand so slow—overhand so sure,
                They do not hasten, each man hits in his place.

[13]   The negro holds firmly the reins of his four horses . . . . the block
                    swags underneath on its tied-over chain,

---

[6]Dances popularized by minstrel shows.

220 The negro that drives the huge dray of the stoneyard . . . . steady
and tall he stands poised on one leg on the stringpiece,
His blue shirt exposes his ample neck and breast and loosens over
his hipband,
His glance is calm and commanding . . . . he tosses the slouch of
his hat away from his forehead,
The sun falls on his crispy hair and moustache . . . . falls on the
black of his polish'd and perfect limbs.

I behold the picturesque giant and love him . . . . and I do not
stop there,
225 I go with the team also.

In me the caresser of life wherever moving . . . . backward as well
as forward slueing,
To niches aside and junior bending.

Oxen that rattle the yoke or halt in the shade, what is that you
express in your eyes?
It seems to me more than all the print I have read in my life.

230 My tread scares the wood-drake and wood-duck on my distant and
daylong ramble,
They rise together, they slowly circle around.
. . . . I believe in those winged purposes,
And acknowledge the red yellow and white playing within me,
And consider the green and violet and the tufted crown
intentional;
235 And do not call the tortoise unworthy because she is not
something else,
And the mockingbird in the swamp never studied the gamut, yet
trills pretty well to me,
And the look of the bay mare shames silliness out of me.

[14] The wild gander leads his flock through the cool night,
Ya-honk! he says, and sounds it down to me like an invitation;
240 The pert may suppose it meaningless, but I listen closer,
I find its purpose and place up there toward the November sky.

The sharphoofed moose of the north, the cat on the housesill, the
chickadee, the prairie-dog,
The litter of the grunting sow as they tug at her teats,
The brood of the turkeyhen, and she with her halfspread wings,
245 I see in them and myself the same old law.

The press of my foot to the earth springs a hundred affections,
They scorn the best I can do to relate them.

I am enamoured of growing outdoors,
Of men that live among cattle or taste of the ocean or woods,
250 Of the builders and steerers of ships, of the wielders of axes and
    mauls, of the drivers of horses,
I can eat and sleep with them week in and week out.

What is commonest and cheapest and nearest and easiest is Me,
Me going in for my chances, spending for vast returns,
Adorning myself to bestow myself on the first that will take me,
255 Not asking the sky to come down to my goodwill,
Scattering it freely forever.

[15]   The pure contralto sings in the organloft,
The carpenter dresses his plank . . . . the tongue of his foreplane
    whistles its wild ascending lisp,
The married and unmarried children ride home to their
    thanksgiving dinner,
260 The pilot seizes the king-pin, he heaves down with a strong arm,
The mate stands braced in the whaleboat, lance and harpoon are
    ready,
The duck-shooter walks by silent and cautious stretches,
The deacons are ordained with crossed hands at the altar,
The spinning-girl retreats and advances to the hum of the big
    wheel,
265 The farmer stops by the bars of a Sunday and looks at the oats
    and rye,
The lunatic is carried at last to the asylum a confirmed case,
He will never sleep any more as he did in the cot in his mother's
    bedroom;
The jour printer with gray head and gaunt jaws works at his case,
He turns his quid of tobacco, his eyes get blurred with the
    manuscript;
270 The malformed limbs are tied to the anatomist's table,
What is removed drops horribly in a pail;
The quadroon girl is sold at the stand . . . . the drunkard nods by
    the barroom stove,
The machinist rolls up his sleeves . . . . the policeman travels his
    beat . . . . the gate-keeper marks who pass,
The young fellow drives the express-wagon . . . . I love him
    though I do not know him;
275 The half-breed straps on his light boots to compete in the race,
The western turkey-shooting draws old and young . . . . some lean
    on their rifles, some sit on logs,
Out from the crowd steps the marksman and takes his position
    and levels his piece;
The groups of newly-come immigrants cover the wharf or levee,
The woollypates hoe in the sugarfield, the overseer views them
    from his saddle;

280 The bugle calls in the ballroom, the gentlemen run for their
    partners, the dancers bow to each other;
The youth lies awake in the cedar-roofed garret and harks to the
    musical rain,
The Wolverine[7] sets traps on the creek that helps fill the Huron,
The reformer ascends the platform, he spouts with his mouth and
    nose,
The company returns from its excursion, the darkey brings up the
    rear and bears the well-riddled target,
285 The squaw wrapt in her yellow-hemmed cloth is offering moccasins
    and beadbags for sale,
The connoisseur peers along the exhibition-gallery with halfshut
    eyes bent sideways,
The deckhands make fast the steamboat, the plank is thrown for
    the shoregoing passengers,
The young sister holds out the skein, the elder sister winds it off
    in a ball and stops now and then for the knots,
The one-year wife is recovering and happy, a week ago she bore
    her first child,
290 The cleanhaired Yankee girl works with her sewing-machine or in
    the factory or mill,
The nine months' gone is in the parturition chamber, her faintness
    and pains are advancing;
The pavingman leans on his twohanded rammer—the reporter's
    lead flies swiftly over the notebook—the signpainter is
    lettering with red and gold,
The canal-boy trots on the towpath—the bookkeeper counts at his
    desk—the shoemaker waxes his thread,
The conductor beats time for the band and all the performers
    follow him,
295 The child is baptised—the convert is making the first professions,
The regatta is spread on the bay . . . . how the white sails sparkle!
The drover watches his drove, he sings out to them that would
    stray,
The pedlar sweats with his pack on his back—the purchaser
    higgles about the odd cent,
The camera and plate are prepared, the lady must sit for her
    daguerreotype,
300 The bride unrumples her white dress, the minutehand of the clock
    moves slowly,
The opium eater reclines with rigid head and just-opened lips,
The prostitute draggles her shawl, her bonnet bobs on her tipsy
    and pimpled neck,
The crowd laugh at her blackguard oaths, the men jeer and wink
    to each other,
(Miserable! I do not laugh at your oaths nor jeer you,)

[7]Inhabitant of Michigan.

305 The President holds a cabinet council, he is surrounded by the
   great secretaries,
On the piazza walk five friendly matrons with twined arms;
The crew of the fish-smack pack repeated layers of halibut in the
   hold,
The Missourian crosses the plains toting his wares and his cattle,
The fare-collector goes through the train—he gives notice by the
   jingling of loose change,
310 The floormen are laying the floor—the tinners are tinning the
   roof—the masons are calling for mortar,
In single file each shouldering his hod pass onward the laborers;
Seasons pursuing each other the indescribable crowd is gathered
   . . . . it is the Fourth of July . . . . what salutes of cannon and
   small arms!
Seasons pursuing each other the plougher ploughs and the mower
   mows and the wintergrain falls in the ground;
Off on the lakes the pikefisher watches and waits by the hole in
   the frozen surface,
315 The stumps stand thick round the clearing, the squatter strikes
   deep with his axe,
The flatboatmen make fast toward dusk near the cottonwood or
   pekantrees,
The coon-seekers go now through the regions of the Red river, or
   through those drained by the Tennessee, or through those of
   the Arkansas,
The torches shine in the dark that hangs on the Chattahoochee or
   Altamahaw;
Patriarchs sit at supper with sons and grandsons and great
   grandsons around them,
320 In walls of adobe, in canvass tents, rest hunters and trappers after
   their day's sport.
The city sleeps and the country sleeps,
The living sleep for their time . . . . the dead sleep for their time,
The old husband sleeps by his wife and the young husband sleeps
   by his wife;
And these one and all tend inward to me, and I tend outward to
   them,
325 And such as it is to be of these more or less I am.

[16]   I am of old and young, of the foolish as much as the wise,
Regardless of others, ever regardful of others,
Maternal as well as paternal, a child as well as a man,
Stuffed with the stuff that is coarse, and stuffed with the stuff that
   is fine,
330 One of the great nation, the nation of many nations—the smallest
   the same and the largest the same,
A southerner soon as a northerner, a planter nonchalant and
   hospitable,

A Yankee bound my own way . . . . ready for trade . . . . my
　　joints the limberest joints on earth and the sternest joints on
　　earth,
A Kentuckian walking the vale of the Elkhorn in my deerskin
　　leggings,
A boatman over the lakes or bays or along coasts . . . . a Hoosier,
　　a Badger, a Buckeye,[8]
335 A Louisianian or Georgian, a poke-easy from sandhills and pines,
At home on Canadian snowshoes or up in the bush, or with
　　fishermen off Newfoundland,
At home in the fleet of iceboats, sailing with the rest and tacking,
At home on the hills of Vermont or in the woods of Maine or the
　　Texan ranch,
Comrade of Californians . . . . comrade of free northwesterners,
　　loving their big proportions,
340 Comrade of raftsmen and coalmen—comrade of all who shake
　　hands and welcome to drink and meat;
A learner with the simplest, a teacher of the thoughtfulest,
A novice beginning experient of myriads of seasons,
Of every hue and trade and rank, of every caste and religion,
Not merely of the New World but of Africa Europe or Asia . . . .
　　a wandering savage,
345 A farmer, mechanic, or artist . . . . a gentleman, sailor, lover or
　　quaker,
A prisoner, fancy-man, rowdy, lawyer, physician or priest.

I resist anything better than my own diversity,
And breathe the air and leave plenty after me,
And am not stuck up, and am in my place.

350 The moth and the fisheggs are in their place,
The suns I see and the suns I cannot see are in their place,
The palpable is in its place and the impalpable is in its place.

[17]　　These are the thoughts of all men in all ages and lands, they are
　　not original with me,
If they are not yours as much as mine they are nothing or next to
　　nothing,
355 If they do not enclose everything they are next to nothing,
If they are not the riddle and the untying of the riddle they are
　　nothing,
If they are not just as close as they are distant they are nothing.

---

[8]Inhabitants of Indiana, Wisconsin, and Ohio
respectively.

This is the grass that grows wherever the land is and the water is,
This is the common air that bathes the globe.

360 This is the breath of laws and songs and behaviour,
This is the tasteless water of souls . . . . this is the true sustenance,
It is for the illiterate . . . . it is for the judges of the supreme court
. . . . it is for the federal capitol and the state capitols,
It is for the admirable communes of literary men and composers
and singers and lecturers and engineers and savans,
It is for the endless races of working people and farmers and
seamen.

365 This is the trill of a thousand clear cornets and scream of the
octave flute and strike of triangles.

[18]   I play not a march for victors only . . . . I play great marches for
conquered and slain persons.

Have you heard that it was good to gain the day?
I also say it is good to fall . . . . battles are lost in the same spirit
in which they are won.

I sound triumphal drums for the dead . . . . I fling through my
embouchures[9] the loudest and gayest music to them,
370 Vivas to those who have failed, and to those whose war-vessels
sank in the sea, and those themselves who sank in the sea,
And to all generals that lost engagements, and all overcome heroes,
and the numberless unknown heroes equal to the greatest
heroes known.

[19]   This is the meal pleasantly set . . . . this is the meat and drink for
natural hunger,
It is for the wicked just the same as the righteous . . . . I make
appointments with all,
I will not have a single person slighted or left away,
375 The keptwoman and sponger and thief are hereby invited . . . . the
heavy-lipped slave is invited. . . . the venerealee is invited,
There shall be no difference between them and the rest.

This is the press of a bashful hand . . . . this is the float and odor
of hair,
This is the touch of my lips to yours . . . . this is the murmur of
yearning,

[9]Another borrowing from the French, suggesting an opening, or a mouthpiece of a musical
instrument.

This is the far-off depth and height reflecting my own face,
380 This is the thoughtful merge of myself and the outlet again.
Do you guess I have some intricate purpose?
Well I have .... for the April rain has, and the mica on the side
    of a rock has.

Do you take it I would astonish?
Does the daylight astonish? or the early redstart twittering through
    the woods?
385 Do I astonish more than they?

This hour I tell things in confidence,
I might not tell everybody but I will tell you.

[20]   Who goes there! hankering, gross, mystical, nude?
How is it I extract strength from the beef I eat?

390 What is a man anyhow? What am I? and what are you?
All I mark as my own you shall offset it with your own,
Else it were time lost listening to me.

I do not snivel that snivel the world over,
That months are vacuums and the ground but wallow and filth,
395 That life is a suck and a sell, and nothing remains at the end but
    threadbare crape and tears.

Whimpering and truckling fold with powders for invalids ....
    conformity goes to the fourth-removed,
I cock my hat as I please indoors or out.

Shall I pray? Shall I venerate and be ceremonious?

I have pried through the strata and analyzed to a hair,
400 And counselled with doctors and calculated close and found no
    sweeter fat than sticks to my own bones.

In all people I see myself, none more and not one a barleycorn
    less,
And the good or bad I say of myself I say of them.

And I know I am solid and sound,
To me the converging objects of the universe perpetually flow,
405 All are written to me, and I must get what the writing means.

And I know I am deathless,
I know this orbit of mine cannot be swept by a carpenter's
    compass,

I know I shall not pass like a child's carlacue cut with a burnt
    stick at night.

I know I am august,
410 I do not trouble my spirit to vindicate itself or be understood,
I see that the elementary laws never apologize,
I reckon I behave no prouder than the level I plant my house by
    after all.

I exist as I am, that is enough,
If no other in the world be aware I sit content,
415 And if each and all be aware I sit content.

One world is aware, and by far the largest to me, and that is
    myself,
And whether I come to my own today or in ten thousand or ten
    million years,
I can cheerfully take it now, or with equal cheerfulness I can wait.

My foothold is tenoned and mortised in granite,
420 I laugh at what you call dissolution,
And I know the amplitude of time.

[21]   I am the poet of the body,
And I am the poet of the soul.

The pleasures of heaven are with me, and the pains of hell are
    with me,
425 The first I graft and increase upon myself . . . . the latter I
    translate into a new tongue.

I am the poet of the woman the same as the man,
And I say it is as great to be a woman as to be a man,
And I say there is nothing greater than the mother of men.
I chant a new chant of dilation or pride,
430 We have had ducking and deprecating about enough,
I show that size is only development.

Have you outstript the rest? Are you the President?
It is a trifle . . . . they will more than arrive there every one, and
    still pass on.

I am he that walks with the tender and growing night;
435 I call to the earth and sea half-held by the night.

Press close barebosomed night! Press close magnetic nourishing
    night!

Night of south winds! Night of the large few stars!
Still nodding night! Mad naked summer night!

Smile O voluptuous coolbreathed earth!
440 Earth of the slumbering and liquid trees!
Earth of departed sunset! Earth of the mountains misty-topt!
Earth of the vitreous pour of the full moon just tinged with blue!
Earth of shine and dark mottling the tide of the river!
Earth of the limpid gray of clouds brighter and clearer for my
        sake!
445 Far-swooping elbowed earth! Rich apple-blossomed earth!
Smile, for your lover comes!

Prodigal! you have given me love! . . . . therefore I to you give
        love!
O unspeakable passionate love!

Thruster holding me tight and that I hold tight!
450 We hurt each other as the bridegroom and the bride hurt each
        other.

[22]   You sea! I resign myself to you also . . . . I guess what you mean,
I behold from the beach your crooked inviting fingers,
I believe you refuse to go back without feeling of me;
We must have a turn together . . . . I undress . . . . hurry me out
        of sight of the land,
455 Cushion me soft . . . . rock me in billowy drowse,
Dash me with amorous wet . . . . I can repay you.

Sea of stretched ground-swells!
Sea breathing broad and convulsive breaths!
Sea of the brine of life! Sea of unshovelled and always-ready
        graves!
460 Howler and scooper of storms! Capricious and dainty sea!
I am integral with you . . . . I too am of one phase and of all
        phases.

Partaker of influx and efflux . . . . extoler of hate and conciliation,
Extoler of amies[10] and those that sleep in each others' arms.

I am he attesting sympathy;

---

[10]French for girlfriend; Whitman probably intended to suggest comrades and lovers of either sex.

465 Shall I make my list of things in the house and skip the house that
     supports them?

I am the poet of commonsense and of the demonstrable and of
     immortality;
And am not the poet of goodness only . . . . I do not decline to
     be the poet of wickedness also.

Washes and razors for foofoos . . . . for me freckles and a bristling
     beard.

What blurt is it about virtue and about vice?
470 Evil propels me, and reform of evil propels me . . . . I stand
     indifferent,
My gait is no faultfinder's or rejecter's gait,
I moisten the roots of all that has grown.

Did you fear some scrofula out of the unflagging pregnancy?
Did you guess the celestial laws are yet to be worked over and
     rectified?

475 I step up to say that what we do is right and what we affirm is
     right . . . . and some is only the ore of right,
Witnesses of us . . . . one side a balance and the antipodal side a
     balance,
Soft doctrine as steady help as stable doctrine,
Thoughts and deeds of the present our rouse and early start.

This minute that comes to me over the past decillions,
480 There is no better than it and now.

What behaved well in the past or behaves well today is not such a
     wonder,
The wonder is always and always how there can be a mean man or
     an infidel.

[23]   Endless unfolding of words of ages!
And mine a word of the modern . . . . a word en masse.

485 A word of the faith that never balks,
One time as good as another time . . . . here or henceforward it is
     all the same to me.

A word of reality . . . . materialism first and last imbueing.

Hurrah for positive science! Long live exact demonstration!
Fetch stonecrop and mix it with cedar and branches of lilac;

490 This is the lexicographer or chemist . . . . this made a grammar of
    the old cartouches,[11]
These mariners put the ship through dangerous unknown seas,
This is the geologist, and this works with the scalpel, and this is a
    mathematician.

Gentlemen I receive you, and attach and clasp hands with you,
The facts are useful and real . . . . they are not my dwelling . . . .
    I enter by them to an area of the dwelling.

495 I am less the reminder of property or qualities, and more the
    reminder of life,
And go on the square for my own sake and for others' sakes,
And make short account of neuters and geldings, and favor men
    and women fully equipped,
And beat the gong of revolt, and stop with fugitives and them that
    plot and conspire.

[24]   Walt Whitman, an American, one of the roughs, a kosmos,
500 Disorderly fleshy and sensual . . . . eating drinking and breeding,
No sentimentalist . . . . no stander above men and women or apart
    from them . . . . no more modest than immodest.

Unscrew the locks from the doors!
Unscrew the doors themselves from their jambs!

Whoever degrades another degrades me . . . . and whatever is
    done or said returns at last to me,
505 And whatever I do or say I also return.

Through me the afflatus[12] surging and surging . . . . through me
    the current and index.

I speak the password primeval . . . . I give the sign of democracy;
By God! I will accept nothing which all cannot have their
    counterpart of on the same terms.

Through me many long dumb voices,
510 Voices of the interminable generations of slaves,
Voices of prostitutes and of deformed persons,
Voices of the diseased and despairing, and of thieves and dwarfs,
Voices of cycles of preparation and accretion,
And of the threads that connect the stars—and of wombs, and of
    the fatherstuff,

[11]Scroll-like tablets used for the inscription of
  Egyptian hieroglyphics.
[12]Creative spirit or divine breath.

515   And of the rights of them the others are down upon,
      Of the trivial and flat and foolish and despised,
      Of fog in the air and beetles rolling balls of dung.

      Through me forbidden voices,
      Voices of sexes and lusts . . . . voices veiled, and I remove the veil,
520   Voices indecent by me clarified and transfigured.
      I do not press my finger across my mouth,
      I keep as delicate around the bowels as around the head and
            heart,
      Copulation is no more rank to me than death is.

      I believe in the flesh and the appetites,
525   Seeing hearing and feeling are miracles, and each part and tag of
            me is a miracle.

      Divine am I inside and out, and I make holy whatever I touch or
            am touched from;
      The scent of these arm-pits is aroma finer than prayer,
      This head is more than churches or bibles or creeds.

      If I worship any particular thing it shall be some of the spread of
            my body;
530   Translucent mould of me it shall be you,
      Shaded ledges and rests, firm masculine coulter,[13] it shall be
            you,
      Whatever goes to the tilth of me it shall be you,
      You my rich blood, your milky stream pale strippings of my life;
      Breast that presses against other breasts it shall be you,
535   My brain it shall be your occult convolutions,
      Root of washed sweet-flag, timorous pond-snipe, nest of guarded
            duplicate eggs, it shall be you,
      Mixed tussled hay of head and beard and brawn it shall be you,
      Trickling sap of maple, fibre of manly wheat, it shall be you;
      Sun so generous it shall be you,
540   Vapors lighting and shading my face it shall be you,
      You sweaty brooks and dews it shall be you,
      Winds whose soft-tickling genitals rub against me it shall be you,
      Broad muscular fields, branches of liveoak, loving lounger in my
            winding paths, it shall be you,
      Hands I have taken, face I have kissed, mortal I have ever
            touched, it shall be you.

545   I dote on myself . . . . there is that lot of me, and all so luscious,
      Each moment and whatever happens thrills me with joy.

[13]The iron blade of a plow.

I cannot tell how my ankles bend . . . . nor whence the cause of
    my faintest wish,
Nor the cause of the friendship I emit . . . . nor the cause of the
    friendship I take again.

To walk up my stoop is unaccountable . . . . I pause to consider if
    it really be,
550 That I eat and drink is spectacle enough for the great authors and
    schools,
A morning-glory at my window satisfies me more than the
    metaphysics of books.

To behold the daybreak!
The little light fades the immense and diaphanous shadows,
The air tastes good to my palate.

555 Hefts of the moving world at innocent gambols, silently rising,
    freshly exuding,
Scooting obliquely high and low.

Something I cannot see puts upward libidinous[14] prongs,
Seas of bright juice suffuse heaven.

The earth by the sky staid with . . . . the daily close of their
    junction,
560 The heaved challenge from the east that moment over my head,
The mocking taunt, See then whether you shall be master!

[25]   Dazzling and tremendous how quick the sunrise would kill me,
If I could not now and always send sunrise out of me.

We also ascend dazzling and tremendous as the sun,
565 We found our own my soul in the calm and cool of the daybreak.

My voice goes after what my eyes cannot reach,
With the twirl of my tongue I encompass worlds and volumes of
    worlds.
Speech is the twin of my vision . . . . it is unequal to measure itself.

It provokes me forever,
570 It says sarcastically, Walt, you understand enough . . . . why don't
    you let it out then?

Come now I will not be tantalized . . . . you conceive too much of
    articulation.

---

[14]Full of sexual energy, desire.

Do you not know how the buds beneath are folded?
Waiting in gloom protected by frost,
The dirt receding before my prophetical screams,
575 I underlying causes to balance them at last,
    My knowledge my live parts . . . . it keeping tally with the
        meaning of things,
    Happiness . . . . which whoever hears me let him or her set out in
        search of this day.

My final merit I refuse you . . . . I refuse putting from me the best
    I am.

Encompass worlds but never try to encompass me,
580 I crowd your noisiest talk by looking toward you.

Writing and talk do not prove me,
I carry the plenum of proof and every thing else in my face,
With the hush of my lips I confound the topmost skeptic.

[26]   I think I will do nothing for a long time but listen,
585 And accrue what I hear into myself . . . . and let sounds
        contribute toward me.

I hear the bravuras of birds . . . . the bustle of growing wheat
    . . . . gossip of flames . . . . clack of sticks cooking my meals.

I hear the sound of the human voice . . . . a sound I love,
I hear all sounds as they are tuned to their uses . . . . sounds of
        the city and sounds out of the city . . . . sounds of the day
        and night;
    Talkative young ones to those that like them . . . . the recitative of
        fish-pedlars and fruit-pedlars . . . . the loud laugh of
        workpeople at their meals,
590 The angry base of disjointed friendship . . . . the faint tones of the
        sick,
    The judge with hands tight to the desk, his shaky lips pronouncing
        a death-sentence,
    The heave'e'yo of stevedores unlading ships by the wharves . . . .
        the refrain of the anchor-lifters;
    The ring of alarm-bells . . . . the cry of fire . . . . the whirr of
        swift-streaking engines and hose-carts with premonitory tinkles
        and colored lights,
    The steam-whistle . . . . the solid roll of the train of approaching
        cars;
595 The slow-march played at night at the head of the association,
    They go to guard some corpse . . . . the flag-tops are draped with
        black muslin.

I hear the violincello or man's heart's complaint,
And hear the keyed cornet or else the echo of sunset.

I hear the chorus . . . . it is a grand-opera . . . . this indeed is
    music!

600 A tenor large and fresh as the creation fills me,
The orbic flex of his mouth is pouring and filling me full.

I hear the trained soprano . . . . she convulses me like the climax
    of my love-grip;
The orchestra whirls me wider than Uranus flies,
It wrenches unnamable ardors from my breast,
605 It throbs me to gulps of the farthest down horror,
It sails me . . . . I dab with bare feet . . . . they are licked by the
    indolent waves,
I am exposed . . . . cut by bitter and poisoned hail,
Steeped amid honeyed morphine . . . . my windpipe squeezed in
    the fakes[15] of death,
Let up again to feel the puzzle of puzzles,
610 And that we call Being.

[27]   To be in any form, what is that?
If nothing lay more developed the quahaug and its callous shell
    were enough.

Mine is no callous shell,
I have instant conductors all over me whether I pass or stop,
615 They seize every object and lead it harmlessly through me.

I merely stir, press, feel with my fingers, and am happy,
To touch my person to some one else's is about as much as I can
    stand.

[28]   Is this then a touch? . . . . quivering me to a new identity,
Flames and ether making a rush for my veins,
620 Treacherous tip of me reaching and crowding to help them,
My flesh and blood playing out lightning, to strike what is hardly
    different from myself,
On all sides prurient provokers stiffening my limbs,
Straining the udder of my heart for its withheld drip,
Behaving licentious toward me, taking no denial,
625 Depriving me of my best as for a purpose,
Unbuttoning my clothes and holding me by the bare waist,

---

[15]Coils of a rope.

Deluding my confusion with the calm of the sunlight and pasture
  fields,
Immodestly sliding the fellow-senses away,
They bribed to swap off with touch, and go and graze at the edges
  of me,
630 No consideration, no regard for my draining strength or my anger,
Fetching the rest of the herd around to enjoy them awhile,
Then all uniting to stand on a headland and worry me.

The sentries desert every other part of me,
They have left me helpless to a red marauder,
635 They all come to the headland to witness and assist against me.
I am given up by traitors;
I talk wildly . . . . I have lost my wits . . . . I and nobody else am
  the greatest traitor,
I went myself first to the headland . . . . my own hands carried me
  there.

You villain touch! what are you doing? . . . . my breath is tight in
  its throat;
640 Unclench your floodgates! you are too much for me.

[29]   Blind loving wrestling touch! Sheathed hooded sharptoothed
          touch!
        Did it make you ache so leaving me?

        Parting tracked by arriving . . . . perpetual payment of the
          perpetual loan,
        Rich showering rain, and recompense richer afterward.

645   Sprouts take and accumulate . . . . stand by the curb prolific and
          vital,
        Landscapes projected masculine full-sized and golden.

[30]   All truths wait in all things,
        They neither hasten their own delivery nor resist it,
        They do not need the obstetric forceps of the surgeon,
650   The insignificant is as big to me as any,
        What is less or more than a touch?

        Logic and sermons never convince,
        The damp of the night drives deeper into my soul.

        Only what proves itself to every man and woman is so,
655   Only what nobody denies is so.

        A minute and a drop of me settle my brain;
        I believe the soggy clods shall become lovers and lamps,

And a compend of compends is the meat of a man or woman,
And a summit and flower there is the feeling they have for each
other,
660 And they are to branch boundlessly out of that lesson until it
becomes omnific,
And until every one shall delight us, and we them.

[31]   I believe a leaf of grass is no less than the journeywork of the
stars,
And the pismire is equally perfect, and a grain of sand, and the
egg of the wren,
And the tree-toad is a chef-d'ouvre[16] for the highest,
665 And the running blackberry would adorn the parlors of heaven,
And the narrowest hinge in my hand puts to scorn all machinery,
And the cow crunching with depressed head surpasses any statue,
And a mouse is miracle enough to stagger sextillions of infidels,
And I could come every afternoon of my life to look at the
farmer's girl boiling her iron tea-kettle and baking shortcake.

670 I find I incorporate gneiss and coal and long-threaded moss and
fruits and grains and esculent roots,
And am stucco'd with quadrupeds and birds all over,
And have distanced what is behind me for good reasons,
And call any thing close again when I desire it.

In vain the speeding or shyness,
675 In vain the plutonic rocks send their old heat against my approach,
In vain the mastadon retreats beneath its own powdered bones,
In vain objects stand leagues off and assume manifold shapes,
In vain the ocean settling in hollows and the great monsters lying
low,
In vain the buzzard houses herself with the sky,
680 In vain the snake slides through the creepers and logs,
In vain the elk takes to the inner passes of the woods,
In vain the razorbilled auk sails far north to Labrador,
I follow quickly . . . . I ascend to the nest in the fissure of the
cliff.

[32]   I think I could turn and live awhile with the animals . . . . they are
so placid and self-contained,
685 I stand and look at them sometimes half the day long.

They do not sweat and whine about their condition,
They do not lie awake in the dark and weep for their sins,

---

[16]Masterpiece.

They do not make me sick discussing their duty to God,
Not one is dissatisfied . . . . not one is demented with the mania
    of owning things,
690 Not one kneels to another nor to his kind that lived thousands of
    years ago,
Not one is respectable or industrious over the whole earth.

So they show their relations to me and I accept them;
They bring me tokens of myself . . . . they evince them plainly in
    their possession.

I do not know where they got those tokens,
695 I must have passed that way untold times ago and negligently
    dropt them,
Myself moving forward then and now and forever,
Gathering and showing more always and with velocity,
Infinite and omnigenous and the like of these among them;
Not too exclusive toward the reachers of my remembrancers,
700 Picking out here one that shall be my amie,
Choosing to go with him on brotherly terms.

A gigantic beauty of a stallion, fresh and responsive to my caresses,
Head high in the forehead and wide between the ears,
Limbs glossy and supple, tail dusting the ground,
705 Eyes well apart and full of sparkling wickedness . . . . ears finely
    cut and flexibly moving.

His nostrils dilate . . . . my heels embrace him . . . . his well built
    limbs tremble with pleasure . . . . we speed around and
    return.
I but use you a moment and then I resign you stallion . . . . and
    do not need your paces, and outgallop them,
And myself as I stand or sit pass faster than you.

[33]   Swift wind! Space! My Soul! Now I know it is true what I guessed
    at;
710 What I guessed when I loafed on the grass,
What I guessed while I lay alone in my bed . . . . and again as I
    walked the beach under the paling stars of the morning.

My ties and ballasts[17] leave me . . . . I travel . . . . I sail . . . . my
    elbows rest in the sea-gaps,
I skirt the sierras . . . . my palms cover continents,
I am afoot with my vision.

[17]As of a hot air balloon.

715 By the city's quadrangular houses .... in log-huts, or camping
    with lumbermen,
Along the ruts of the turnpike .... along the dry gulch and
    rivulet bed,
Hoeing my onion-patch, and rows of carrots and parsnips ....
    crossing savannas ... trailing in forests,
Prospecting .... gold-digging .... girdling the trees of a new
    purchase,
Scorched ankle-deep by the hot sand .... hauling my boat down
    the shallow river;
720 Where the panther walks to and fro on a limb overhead ....
    where the buck turns furiously at the hunter,
Where the rattlesnake suns his flabby length on a rock .... where
    the otter is feeding on fish,
Where the alligator in his tough pimples sleeps by the bayou,
Where the black bear is searching for roots or honey .... where
    the beaver pats the mud with his paddle-tail;
Over the growing sugar .... over the cottonplant .... over the
    rice in its low moist field;
725 Over the sharp-peaked farmhouse with its scalloped scum and
    slender shoots from the gutters;
Over the western persimmon .... over the longleaved corn and
    the delicate blueflowered flax;
Over the white and brown buckwheat, a hummer and a buzzer
    there with the rest,
Over the dusky green of the rye as it ripples and shades in the
    breeze;
Scaling mountains .... pulling myself cautiously up .... holding
    on by low scragged limbs,
730 Walking the path worn in the grass and beat through the leaves of
    the brush;
Where the quail is whistling betwixt the woods and the wheatlot,
Where the bat flies in the July eve .... where the great goldbug
    drops through the dark;
Where the flails keep time on the barn floor,
Where the brook puts out of the roots of the old tree and flows to
    the meadow,
735 Where cattle stand and shake away flies with the tremulous
    shuddering of their hides,
Where the cheese-cloth hangs in the kitchen, and andirons straddle
    the hearth-slab, and cobwebs fall in festoons from the rafters;
Where triphammers crash .... where the press is whirling its
    cylinders;
Wherever the human heart beats with terrible throes out of its
    ribs:
Where the pear-shaped balloon is floating aloft .... floating in it
    myself and looking composedly down:

740 Where the life-car[18] is drawn on the slipnoose . . . . where the
    heat hatches pale-green eggs in the dented sand,
Where the she-whale swims with her calves and never forsakes
    them,
Where the steamship trails hindways its long pennant of smoke,
Where the ground-shark's fin cuts like a black chip out of the
    water,
Where the half-burned brig is riding on unknown currents,
745 Where shells grow to her slimy deck, and the dead are corrupting
    below;
Where the striped and starred flag is borne at the head of the
    regiments;
Approaching Manhattan, up by the long-stretching island,
Under Niagara, the cataract falling like a veil over my
    countenance;
Upon a door-step . . . . upon the horse-block of hard wood
    outside,
750 Upon the race-course, or enjoying pic-nics or jigs or a good game
    of base-ball,
At he-festivals with blackguard jibes and ironical license and bull-
    dances and drinking and laughter,
At the cider-mill, tasting the sweet of the brown sqush[19]. . . .
    sucking the juice through a straw,
At apple-pealings, wanting kisses for all the red fruit I find,
At musters[20] and beach-parties and friendly bees and huskings and
    house-raisings;
755 Where the mockingbird sounds his delicious gurgles, and cackles
    and screams and weeps,
Where the hay-rick stands in the barnyard, and the dry-stalks are
    scattered, and the brood cow waits in the hovel,
Where the bull advances to do his masculine work, and the stud
    to the mare, and the cock is treading the hen,
Where the heifers browse, and the geese nip their food with short
    jerks;
Where the sundown shadows lengthen over the limitless and
    lonesome prairie,
760 Where the herds of buffalo make a crawling spread of the square
    miles far and near;
Where the hummingbird shimmers . . . . where the neck of the
    longlived swan is curving and winding;
Where the laughing-gull scoots by the slappy shore and laughs her
    near-human laugh;
Where beehives range on a gray bench in the garden half-hid by
    the high weeds;

[18]A water-tight rescue vessel used to save passenger at sea.

[19]Mush.
[20]Gatherings of people.

Where the band-necked partridges roost in a ring on the ground
    with their heads out;
765 Where burial coaches enter the arched gates of a cemetery;
Where winter wolves bark amid wastes of snow and icicled trees;
Where the yellow-crowned heron comes to the edge of the marsh
    at night and feeds upon small crabs;
Where the splash of swimmers and divers cools the warm noon;
Where the katydid works her chromatic reed on the walnut-tree
    over the well;
770 Through patches of citrons and cucumbers with silver-wired leaves,
Through the salt-lick or orange glade . . . . or under conical firs;
Through the gymnasium . . . . through the curtained saloon . . . .
    through the office or public hall;
Pleased with the native and pleased with the foreign . . . . pleased
    with the new and old,
Pleased with women, the homely as well as the handsome,
775 Pleased with the quakeress as she puts off her bonnet and talks
    melodiously,
Pleased with the primitive tunes of the choir of the whitewashed
    church,
Pleased with the earnest words of the sweating Methodist preacher,
    or any preacher . . . . looking seriously at the camp-meeting;
Looking in at the shop-windows in Broadway the whole forenoon
    . . . . pressing the flesh of my nose to the thick plate-glass,
Wandering the same afternoon with my face turned up to the
    clouds;
780 My right and left arms round the sides of two friends and I in the
    middle;
Coming home with the bearded and dark-cheeked bush-boy . . . .
    riding behind him at the drape of the day;
Far from the settlements studying the print of animals' feet, or the
    moccasin print;
By the cot in the hospital reaching lemonade to a feverish patient,
By the coffined corpse when all is still, examining with a candle;
785 Voyaging to every port to dicker and adventure;
Hurrying with the modern crowd, as eager and fickle as any,
Hot toward one I hate, ready in my madness to knife him;
Solitary at midnight in my back yard, my thoughts gone from me a
    long while,
Walking the old hills of Judea with the beautiful gentle god by my
    side;
790 Speeding through space . . . . speeding through heaven and the
    stars,
Speeding amid the seven satellites and the broad ring and the
    diameter of eighty thousand miles,
Speeding with tailed meteors . . . . throwing fire-balls like the rest,
Carrying the crescent child that carries its own full mother in its
    belly;

Storming enjoying planning loving cautioning,
795 Backing and filling, appearing and disappearing,
    I tread day and night such roads.

I visit the orchards of God and look at the spheric product,
    And look at quintillions ripened, and look at quintillions green.

I fly the flight of the fluid and swallowing soul,
800 My course runs below the soundings of plummets.

I help myself to material and immaterial,
    No guard can shut me off, no law can prevent me.

I anchor my ship for a little while only,
    My messengers continually cruise away or bring their returns to
        me.

805 I go hunting polar furs and the seal . . . . leaping chasms with a
        pike-pointed staff . . . . clinging to topples[21] of brittle and
        blue.

I ascend to the foretruck . . . . I take my place late at night in the
        crow's nest . . . . we sail through the arctic sea . . . . it is
        plenty light enough,
Through the clear atmosphere I stretch around on the wonderful
        beauty,
The enormous masses of ice pass me and I pass them . . . . the
        scenery is plain in all directions,
The white-topped mountains point up in the distance . . . . I fling
        out my fancies toward them;
810 We are about approaching some great battlefield in which we are
        soon to be engaged,
We pass the colossal outposts of the encampments . . . . we pass
        with still feet and caution;
Or we are entering by the suburbs some vast and ruined city . . . .
        the blocks and fallen architecture more than all the living
        cities of the globe.

I am a free companion . . . . I bivouac by invading watchfires.

I turn the bridegroom out of bed and stay with the bride myself,
815 And tighten her all night to my thighs and lips.

My voice is the wife's voice, the screech by the rail of the stairs,
    They fetch my man's body up dripping and drowned.

---

[21]Pieces of ice.

I understand the large hearts of heroes,
The courage of present times and all times;
820 How the skipper[22] saw the crowded and rudderless wreck of the
    steamship, and death chasing it up and down the storm,
How he knuckled tight and gave not back one inch, and was
    faithful of days and faithful of nights,
And chalked in large letters on a board, Be of good cheer, We will
    not desert you;
How he saved the drifting company at last,
How the lank loose-gowned women looked when boated from the
    side of their prepared graves,
825 How the silent old-faced infants, and the lifted sick, and the sharp-
    lipped unshaved men;
All this I swallow and it tastes good . . . . I like it well, and it
    becomes mine,
I am the man . . . . I suffered . . . . I was there.

The disdain and calmness of martyrs,
The mother condemned for a witch and burnt with dry wood, and
    her children gazing on;
830 The hounded slave that flags in the race and leans by the fence,
    blowing and covered with sweat,
The twinges that sting like needles his legs and neck,
The murderous buckshot and the bullets,
All these I feel or am.

I am the hounded slave . . . . I wince at the bite of the dogs,
835 Hell and despair are upon me . . . . crack and again crack the
    marksmen,
I clutch the rails of the fence . . . . my gore dribs[23] thinned with
    the ooze of my skin,
I fall on the weeds and stones,
The riders spur their unwilling horses and haul close,
They taunt my dizzy ears . . . . they beat me violently over the
    head with their whip-stocks.

840 Agonies are one of my changes of garments;
I do not ask the wounded person how he feels . . . . I myself
    become the wounded person,
My hurt turns livid upon me as I lean on a cane and observe.

I am the mashed fireman with breastbone broken . . . . tumbling
    walls buried me in their debris,

[22]Whitman describes the shipwreck of the *San Francisco,* which was reported in the *New York Weekly Tribune* on January 21, 1854; he kept a copy of this article among his belongings.
[23]Short for dribbles.

Heat and smoke I inspired . . . . I heard the yelling shouts of my
    comrades,
845 I heard the distant click of their picks and shovels;
They have cleared the beams away . . . . they tenderly lift me
    forth.

I lie in the night air in my red shirt . . . . the pervading hush is
    for my sake,
Painless after all I lie, exhausted but not so unhappy,
White and beautiful are the faces around me . . . . the heads are
    bared of their fire-caps,
850 The kneeling crowd fades with the light of the torches.

Distant and dead resuscitate,
They show as the dial or move as the hands of me . . . . and I am
    the clock myself.
I am an old artillerist, and tell of some fort's bombardment . . . .
    and am there again.

Again the reveille of drummers . . . . again the attacking cannon
    and mortars and howitzers,
855 Again the attacked send their cannon responsive.

I take part . . . . I see and hear the whole,
The cries and curses and roar . . . . the plaudits for well aimed
    shots,
The ambulanza slowly passing and trailing its red drip,
Workmen searching after damages and to make indispensible
    repairs,
860 The fall of grenades through the rent roof . . . . the fan-shaped
    explosion,
The whizz of limbs heads stone wood and iron high in the air.

Again gurgles the mouth of my dying general . . . . he furiously
    waves with his hand,
He gasps through the clot . . . . Mind not me . . . . mind . . . .
    the entrenchments.

[34]   I tell not the fall of Alamo . . . . not one escaped to tell the fall of
    Alamo,
865 The hundred and fifty are dumb yet at Alamo.

Hear now the tale of a jetblack sunrise,
Hear of the murder in cold blood of four hundred and twelve
    young men.[24]

[24]Whitman tells the story of the death of Captain Fannin and his company of 371 Texans at the hands of the Mexicans after their surrender at Goliad on March 27, 1836; unlike Emerson and Thoreau, Whitman supported the Mexican War (1846–1848).

Retreating they had formed in a hollow square with their baggage
    for breastworks,
Nine hundred lives out of the surrounding enemy's nine times
    their number was the price they took in advance,
870 Their colonel was wounded and their ammunition gone,
They treated for an honorable capitulation, received writing and
    seal, gave up their arms, and marched back prisoners of war.
They were the glory of the race of rangers,
Matchless with a horse, a rifle, a song, a supper, or a courtship,
Large, turbulent, brave, handsome, generous, proud and
    affectionate,
875 Bearded, sunburnt, dressed in the free costume of hunters,
Not a single one over thirty years of age.

The second Sunday morning they were brought out in squads and
    massacred . . . . it was beautiful early summer,
The work commenced about five o'clock and was over by eight.

None obeyed the command to kneel,
880 Some made a mad and helpless rush . . . . some stood stark and
    straight,
A few fell at once, shot in the temple or heart . . . . the living and
    dead lay together,
The maimed and mangled dug in the dirt . . . . the new-comers
    saw them there;
Some half-killed attempted to crawl away,
These were dispatched with bayonets or battered with the blunts
    of muskets;
885 A youth not seventeen years old seized his assassin till two more
    came to release him,
The three were all torn, and covered with the boy's blood.

At eleven o'clock began the burning of the bodies;
And that is the tale of the murder of the four hundred and twelve
    young men,
And that was a jetblack sunrise.

[35]   890 Did you read in the seabooks of the oldfashioned frigate-fight?[25]
Did you learn who won by the light of the moon and stars?

Our foe was no skulk in his ship, I tell you,
His was the English pluck, and there is no tougher or truer, and
    never was, and never will be;

---

[25]Whitman tells the story of the Revolutionary
sea battle on September 23, 1779, between
the *Bonhomme Richard,* commanded by John
Paul Jones, and the British *Serapis.*

Along the lowered eve he came, horribly raking us.
895 We closed with him .... the yards entangled .... the cannon
    touched,
My captain lashed fast with his own hands.

We had received some eighteen-pound shots under the water,
On our lower-gun-deck two large pieces had burst at the first fire,
    killing all around and blowing up overhead.

Ten o'clock at night, and the full moon shining and the leaks on
    the gain, and five feet of water reported,
900 The master-at-arms loosing the prisoners confined in the after-hold
    to give them a chance for themselves.

The transit to and from the magazine was now stopped by the
    sentinels,
They saw so many strange faces they did not know whom to trust.

Our frigate was afire .... the other asked if we demanded
    quarters? if our colors were struck and the fighting done?

I laughed content when I heard the voice of my little captain,
905 We have not struck, he composedly cried, We have just begun our
    part of the fighting.

Only three guns were in use,
One was directed by the captain himself against the enemy's
    mainmast,
Two well-served with grape and canister silenced his musketry and
    cleared his decks.

The tops alone seconded the fire of this little battery, especially the
    maintop,
910 They all held out bravely during the whole of the action.

Not a moment's cease,
The leaks gained fast on the pumps .... the fire eat toward the
    powder-magazine,
One of the pumps was shot away .... it was generally thought we
    were sinking.
Serene stood the little captain,
915 He was not hurried .... his voice was neither high nor low,
His eyes gave more light to us than our battle-lanterns.

Toward twelve at night, there in the beams of the moon they
    surrendered to us.

[36]   Stretched and still lay the midnight,
Two great hulls motionless on the breast of the darkness,
920 Our vessel riddled and slowly sinking . . . . preparations to pass to
     the one we had conquered,
The captain on the quarter deck coldly giving his orders through a
     countenance white as a sheet,
Near by the corpse of the child that served in the cabin,
The dead face of an old salt with long white hair and carefully
     curled whiskers,
The flames spite of all that could be done flickering aloft and
     below,
925 The husky voices of the two or three officers yet fit for duty,
Formless stacks of bodies and bodies by themselves . . . . dabs of
     flesh upon the masts and spars,
The cut of cordage and dangle of rigging . . . . the slight shock of
     the soothe of waves,
Black and impassive guns, and litter of powder-parcels, and the
     strong scent,
Delicate sniffs of the seabreeze . . . . smells of sedgy grass and
     fields by the shore . . . death-messages given in charge to
     survivors,
930 The hiss of the surgeon's knife and the gnawing teeth of his saw,
The wheeze, the cluck, the swash of falling blood . . . . the short
     wild scream, the long dull tapering groan,
These so . . . . these irretrievable.

[37]   O Christ! My fit is mastering me!
What the rebel said gaily adjusting his throat to the rope-noose,
935 What the savage at the stump, his eye-sockets empty, his mouth
     spirting whoops and defiance,
What stills the traveler come to the vault at Mount Vernon,
What sobers the Brooklyn boy as he looks down the shores of the
     Wallabout and remembers the prison ships,[26]
What burnt the gums of the redcoat at Saratoga[27] when he
     surrendered his brigades,
These become mine and me every one, and they are but little,
940 I become as much more as I like.

I become any presence or truth of humanity here,
And see myself in prison shaped like another man,
And feel the dull unintermitted pain.

---

[26]British prison ships along Wallabout Bay, where American rebels were held captive during the Revolutionary War.
[27]On October 17, 1777, the British General Burgoyne surrendered to American forces at Saratoga; the battle was a turning point because it enlisted French assistance for the American cause.

For me the keepers of convicts shoulder their carbines and keep
    watch,
945 It is I let out in the morning and barred at night.

Not a mutineer walks handcuffed to the jail, but I am handcuffed
    to him and walk by his side,
I am less the jolly one there, and more the silent one with sweat
    on my twitching lips.
Not a youngster is taken for larceny, but I go up too and am tried
    and sentenced.

Not a cholera patient lies at the last gasp, but I also lie at the last
    gasp,
950 My face is ash-colored, my sinews gnarl . . . . away from me people
    retreat.

Askers embody themselves in me, and I am embodied in them,
I project my hat and sit shamefaced and beg.

I rise extatic through all, and sweep with the true gravitation,
The whirling and whirling is elemental within me.

[38] 955 Somehow I have been stunned. Stand back!
Give me a little time beyond my cuffed head and slumbers and
    dreams and gaping,
I discover myself on a verge of the usual mistake.

That I could forget the mockers and insults!
That I could forget the trickling tears and the blows of the
    bludgeons and hammers!
960 That I could look with a separate look on my own crucifixion and
    bloody crowning!

I remember . . . . I resume the overstaid fraction,[28]
The grave of rock multiplies what has been confided to it . . . . or
    to any graves,
The corpses rise . . . . the gashes heal . . . . the fastenings roll
    away.

I troop forth replenished with supreme power, one of an average
    unending procession,
965 We walk the roads of Ohio and Massachusetts and Virginia and
    Wisconsin and New York and New Orleans and Texas and

[28]Whitman's meaning is unclear. The reference may be temporal, alluding to the poet's having stayed too long among scenes of suffering and pain. But the words may also allude to Christ as the "overstaid fraction" that the poet "resumes" as a living power within himself.

Montreal and San Francisco and Charleston and Savannah and
Mexico,
Inland and by the seacoast and boundary lines . . . . and we pass
the boundary lines.
Our swift ordinances are on their way over the whole earth,
The blossoms we wear in our hats are the growth of two thousand
years.

Eleves[29] I salute you,
970 I see the approach of your numberless gangs . . . . I see you
understand yourselves and me,
And know that they who have eyes are divine, and the blind and
lame are equally divine,
And that my steps drag behind yours yet go before them,
And are aware how I am with you no more than I am with
everybody.

[39]   The friendly and flowing savage . . . . Who is he?
975 Is he waiting for civilization or past it and mastering it?

Is he some southwesterner raised outdoors? Is he Canadian?
Is he from the Mississippi country? or from Iowa, Oregon or
California? or from the mountains? or prairie life or bush-life?
or from the sea?
Wherever he goes men and women accept and desire him,
They desire he should like them and touch them and speak to
them and stay with them.

980 Behaviour lawless as snow-flakes . . . . words simple as grass . . . .
uncombed head and laughter and naivete;
Slowstepping feet and the common features, and the common
modes and emanations,
They descend in new forms from the tips of his fingers,
They are wafted with the odor of his body or breath . . . . they fly
out of the glance of his eyes.

[40]   Flaunt of the sunshine I need not your bask . . . . lie over,
985 You light surfaces only . . . . I force the surfaces and the depths
also.

Earth! you seem to look for something at my hands,
Say old topknot! what do you want?

Man or woman! I might tell how I like you, but cannot,
And might tell what it is in me and what it is in you, but cannot,

---

[29]French for students.

990 And might tell the pinings I have . . . . the pulse of my nights and
      days.

Behold I do not give lectures or a little charity,
What I give I give out of myself.

You there, impotent, loose in the knees, open your scarfed chops
      till I blow grit within you,
Spread your palms and lift the flaps of your pockets,
995 I am not to be denied . . . . I compel . . . . I have stores plenty
      and to spare,
And any thing I have I bestow.

I do not ask who you are . . . . that is not important to me,
You can do nothing and be nothing but what I will infold you.

To a drudge of the cottonfields or emptier of privies I lean . . . .
      on his right cheek I put the family kiss,
1000 And in my soul I swear I never will deny him.
On women fit for conception I start bigger and nimbler babes,
This day I am jetting the stuff of far more arrogant republics.

To any one dying . . . . thither I speed and twist the knob of the
      door,
Turn the bedclothes toward the foot of the bed,
1005 Let the physician and the priest go home.

I seize the descending man . . . . I raise him with resistless will.

O despairer, here is my neck,
By God! you shall not go down! Hang your whole weight upon me.

I dilate you with tremendous breath . . . . I buoy you up;
1010 Every room of the house do I fill with an armed force . . . . lovers
      of me, bafflers of graves:
Sleep! I and they keep guard all night;
Not doubt, not decease shall dare to lay finger upon you,
I have embraced you, and henceforth possess you to myself,
And when you rise in the morning you will find what I tell you is
      so.

[41] 1015 I am he bringing help for the sick as they pant on their backs,
And for strong upright men I bring yet more needed help.

I heard what was said of the universe,
Heard it and heard of several thousand years;
It is middling well as far as it goes . . . . but is that all?

1020 Magnifying and applying come I,
    Outbidding at the start the old cautious hucksters,
    The most they offer for mankind and eternity less than a spirt of
        my own seminal wet,
    Taking myself the exact dimensions of Jehovah and laying them
        away,
    Lithographing Kronos and Zeus his son, and Hercules his
        grandson,
1025 Buying drafts of Osiris and Isis and Belus and Brahma and
        Adonai,
    In my portfolio placing Manito loose, and Allah on a leaf, and the
        crucifix engraved,
    With Odin, and the hideous-faced Mexitli, and all idols and
        images,[30]
    Honestly taking them all for what they are worth, and not a cent
        more,
    Admitting they were alive and did the work of their day,
1030 Admitting they bore mites as for unfledged birds who have now to
        rise and fly and sing for themselves,
    Accepting the rough deific sketches to fill out better in myself
        .... bestowing them freely on each man and woman I see,
    Discovering as much or more in a framer framing a house,
    Putting higher claims for him there with his rolled-up sleeves,
        driving the mallet and chisel;
    Not objecting to special revelations .... considering a curl of
        smoke or a hair on the back of my hand as curious as any
        revelation;
1035 Those ahold of fire-engines and hook-and-ladder ropes more to me
        than the gods of the antique wars,
    Minding their voices peal through the crash of destruction,
    Their brawny limbs passing safe over charred laths .... their
        white foreheads whole and unhurt out of the flames;
    By the mechanic's wife with her babe at her nipple interceding for
        every person born;
    Three scythes at harvest whizzing in a row from three lusty angels
        with shirts bagged out at their waists;
1040 The snag-toothed hostler with red hair redeeming sins past and to
        come,
    Selling all he possesses and traveling on foot to fee lawyers for his
        brother and sit by him while he is tried for forgery:
    What was strewn in the amplest strewing the square rod about me,
        and not filling the square rod then;

[30]Whitman's list of gods includes sacred figures from several different religions: Jehovah (the Jewish and Christian God); Kronos, Zeus, and Hercules (Greek gods); Osiris and Isis (Egyptian fertility gods); Belus (a legendary Assyrian king); Brahma (the supreme Hindu spirit); Adonai (Lord, in Judaism); Manito (an Algonkian Indian spirit); Allah (Moslem god); Odin (a Danish god of war); Mexitli (an Aztec Indian god of war).

The bull and the bug never worshipped half enough,
Dung and dirt more admirable than was dreamed,
1045 The supernatural of no account . . . . myself waiting my time to be
      one of the supremes,
The day getting ready for me when I shall do as much good as the
      best, and be as prodigious,
Guessing when I am it will not tickle me much to receive puffs
      out of pulpit or print;
By my life-lumps! becoming already a creator!
Putting myself here and now to the ambushed womb of the
      shadows!

[42]   1050 . . . . A call in the midst of the crowd,
My own voice, orotund sweeping and final.

Come my children,
Come my boys and girls, and my women and household and
      intimates,
Now the performer launches his nerve . . . . he has passed his
      prelude on the reeds within.

1055 Easily written loosefingered chords! I feel the thrum of their
      climax and close.

My head evolves on my neck,
Music rolls, but not from the organ . . . . folks are around me, but
      they are no household of mine.

Ever the hard and unsunk ground,
Ever the eaters and drinkers . . . . ever the upward and downward
      sun . . . . ever the air and the ceaseless tides,
1060 Ever myself and my neighbors, refreshing and wicked and real,
Ever the old inexplicable query . . . . ever that thorned thumb—
      that breath of itches and thirsts,
Ever the vexer's hoot! hoot! till we find where the sly one hides
      and bring him forth;
Ever love . . . . ever the sobbing liquid of life,
Ever the bandage under the chin . . . . ever the tressels of death.

1065 Here and there with dimes on the eyes walking,
To feed the greed of the belly the brains liberally spooning,
Tickets buying or taking or selling, but in to the feast never once
      going;
Many sweating and ploughing and thrashing, and then the chaff
      for payment receiving,
A few idly owning, and they the wheat continually claiming.

1070 This is the city . . . . and I am one of the citizens;
　　Whatever interests the rest interests me . . . . politics, churches,
　　　　newspapers, schools,
　　Benevolent societies, improvements, banks, tariffs, steamships,
　　　　factories, markets,
　　Stocks and stores and real estate and personal estate.

　　They who piddle and patter here in collars and tailed coats I
　　　　am aware who they are . . . . and that they are not worms or
　　　　fleas,
1075 I acknowledge the duplicates of myself under all the scrape-lipped
　　　　and pipe-legged concealments.

　　The weakest and shallowest is deathless with me,
　　What I do and say the same waits for them,
　　Every thought that flounders in me the same flounders in them.

　　I know perfectly well my own egotism,
1080 And know my omniverous words, and cannot say any less,
　　And would fetch you whoever you are flush with myself.

　　My words are words of a questioning, and to indicate reality;
　　This printed and bound book . . . . but the printer and the
　　　　printing-office boy?
　　The marriage estate and settlement . . . . but the body and mind
　　　　of the bridegroom? also those of the bride?
1085 The panorama of the sea . . . . but the sea itself?
　　The well-taken photographs . . . . but your wife or friend close
　　　　and solid in your arms?
　　The fleet of ships of the line and all the modern improvements
　　　　. . . . but the craft and pluck of the admiral?
　　The dishes and fare and furniture . . . . but the host and hostess,
　　　　and the look out of their eyes?
　　The sky up there . . . . yet here or next door or across the way?
1090 The saints and sages in history . . . . but you yourself?
　　Sermons and creeds and theology . . . . but the human brain, and
　　　　what is called reason, and what is called love and what is
　　　　called life?

[43]　　I do not despise you priests;
　　My faith is the greatest of faiths and the least of faiths,
　　Enclosing all worship ancient and modern, and all between ancient
　　　　and modern,
1095 Believing I shall come again upon the earth after five thousand
　　　　years,
　　Waiting responses from oracles . . . . honoring the gods . . . .
　　　　saluting the sun,

Making a fetish of the first rock or stump . . . . powowing with
  sticks in the circle of obis,³¹
Helping the lama³² or brahmin as he trims the lamps of the idols,
Dancing yet through the streets in a phallic procession . . . . rapt
  and austere in the woods, a gymnosophist,³³
1100 Drinking mead from the skull-cup . . . . to shasta and vedas
  admirant . . . . minding the koran,³⁴
Walking the teokallis,³⁵ spotted with gore from the stone and
  knife—beating the serpent-skin drum;
Accepting the gospels, accepting him that was crucified, knowing
  assuredly that he is divine,
To the mass kneeling—to the puritan's prayer rising—sitting
  patiently in a pew,
Ranting and frothing in my insane crisis—waiting dead-like till my
  spirit arouses me;
1105 Looking forth on pavement and land, and outside of pavement and
  land,
Belonging to the winders of the circuit of circuits.

One of that centripetal and centrifugal gang,
I turn and talk like a man leaving charges before a journey.
Down-hearted doubters, dull and excluded,
1110 Frivolous sullen moping angry affected disheartened atheistical,
I know every one of you, and know the unspoken interrogatories,
By experience I know them.

How the flukes splash!
How they contort rapid as lightning, with spasms and spouts of
  blood!

1115 Be at peace bloody flukes of doubters and sullen mopers,
I take my place among you as much as among any;
The past is the push of you and me and all precisely the same,
And the night is for you and me and all,
And what is yet untried and afterward is for you and me and all.

1120 I do not know what is untried and afterward,
But I know it is sure and alive, and sufficient.

Each who passes is considered, and each who stops is considered,
  and not a single one can it fail.

---

³¹Sorcery, of African origin, practiced by blacks in the British West Indies and in the American south.
³²Tibetan high priest; brahmin, Hindu high priest.
³³Member of an ancient sect of naked Hindu ascetics.
³⁴Shasta and *vedas,* Hindu sacred texts; the *Koran,* the sacred text of Islam.
³⁵An Aztec temple.

It cannot fail the young man who died and was buried,
Nor the young woman who died and was put by his side,
1125 Nor the little child that peeped in at the door and then drew back
    and was never seen again,
Nor the old man who has lived without purpose, and feels it with
    bitterness worse than gall,
Nor him in the poorhouse tubercled by rum and the bad disorder,
Nor the numberless slaughtered and wrecked . . . . nor the brutish
    koboo,[36] called the ordure of humanity,
Nor the sacs merely floating with open mouths for food to slip in,
1130 Nor any thing in the earth, or down in the oldest graves of the
    earth,
Nor any thing in the myriads of spheres, nor one of the myriads of
    myriads that inhabit them,
Nor the present, nor the least wisp that is known.

[44]   It is time to explain myself . . . . let us stand up.

What is known I strip away . . . . I launch all men and women

    forward with me into the unknown.
1135 The clock indicates the moment . . . . but what does eternity
    indicate?

Eternity lies in bottomless reservoirs . . . . its buckets are rising
    forever and ever,
They pour and they pour and they exhale away.

We have thus far exhausted trillions of winters and summers;
There are trillions ahead, and trillions ahead of them.

1140 Births have brought us richness and variety,
And other births will bring us richness and variety.

I do not call one greater and one smaller,
That which fills its period and place is equal to any.

Were mankind murderous or jealous upon you my brother or my
    sister?
1145 I am sorry for you . . . . they are not murderous or jealous upon
    me;
All has been gentle with me . . . . I keep no account with
    lamentation;
What have I to do with lamentation?

[36]Native of Sumatra.

I am an acme of things accomplished, and I am encloser of things
    to be.

My feet strike an apex of the apices of the stairs,
1150 On every step bunches of ages, and larger bunches between the
    steps,
All below duly traveled—and still I mount and mount.

Rise after rise bow the phantoms behind me,
Afar down I see the huge first Nothing, the vapor from the nostrils
    of death,
I know I was even there . . . . I waited unseen and always,
1155 And slept while God carried me through the lethargic mist,
And took my time . . . . and took no hurt from the foetid carbon.

Long I was hugged close . . . . long and long.

Immense have been the preparations for me,
Faithful and friendly the arms that have helped me.

1160 Cycles ferried my cradle, rowing and rowing like cheerful boatmen;
For room to me stars kept aside in their own rings,
They sent influences to look after what was to hold me.

Before I was born out of my mother generations guided me,
My embryo has never been torpid . . . . nothing could overlay it;
1165 For it the nebula cohered to an orb . . . . the long slow strata
    piled to rest it on . . . . vast vegetables gave it sustenance,
Monstrous sauroids[37] transported it in their mouths and deposited
    it with care.

All forces have been steadily employed to complete and delight me,
Now I stand on this spot with my soul.

[45]   Span of youth! Ever-pushed elasticity! Manhood balanced and
    florid and full!

1170 My lovers suffocate me!
Crowding my lips, and thick in the pores of my skin,
Jostling me through streets and public halls . . . . coming naked to
    me at night,
Crying by day Ahoy from the rocks of the river . . . . swinging and
    chirping over my head,
Calling my name from flowerbeds or vines or tangled underbrush,

[37]Prehistoric reptiles.

1175 Or while I swim in the bath . . . . or drink from the pump at the
     corner . . . . or the curtain is down at the opera . . . . or I
     glimpse at a woman's face in the railroad car;
Lighting on every moment of my life,
Bussing[38] my body with soft and balsamic busses,
Noiselessly passing handfuls out of their hearts and giving them to
     be mine.

Old age superbly rising! Ineffable grace of dying days!

1180 Every condition promulges not only itself . . . . it promulges what
     grows after and out of itself,
And the dark hush promulges as much as any.

I open my scuttle at night and see the far-sprinkled systems,
And all I see, multiplied as high as I can cipher, edge but the rim
     of the farther systems.

Wider and wider they spread, expanding and always expanding,
1185 Outward and outward and forever outward.

My sun has his sun, and round him obediently wheels,
He joins with his partners a group of superior circuit,
And greater sets follow, making specks of the greatest inside them.

There is no stoppage, and never can be stoppage;
1190 If I and you and the worlds and all beneath or upon their
     surfaces, and all the palpable life, were this moment reduced
     back to a pallid float, it would not avail in the long run,
We should surely bring up again where we now stand,
And as surely go as much farther, and then farther and farther.

A few quadrillions of eras, a few octillions of cubic leagues, do not
     hazard the span, or make it impatient,
They are but parts . . . . any thing is but a part.

1195 See ever so far . . . . there is limitless space outside of that,
Count ever so much . . . . there is limitless time around that.
Our rendezvous is fitly appointed . . . . God will be there and wait
     till we come.

[46]   I know I have the best of time and space—and that I was never
     measured, and never will be measured.

---

[38]Kissing.

I tramp a perpetual journey,
1200 My signs are a rain-proof coat and good shoes and a staff cut from
      the woods;
No friend of mine takes his ease in my chair,
I have no chair, nor church nor philosophy;
I lead no man to a dinner-table or library or exchange,
But each man and each woman of you I lead upon a knoll,
1205 My left hand hooks you round the waist,
My right hand points to landscapes of continents, and a plain
      public road.

Not I, not any one else can travel that road for you,
You must travel it for yourself.

It is not far . . . . it is within reach,
1210 Perhaps you have been on it since you were born, and did not
      know,
Perhaps it is every where on water and on land.

Shoulder your duds, and I will mine, and let us hasten forth;
Wonderful cities and free nations we shall fetch as we go.

If you tire, give me both burdens, and rest the chuff of your hand
      on my hip,
1215 And in due time you shall repay the same service to me;
For after we start we never lie by again.

This day before dawn I ascended a hill and looked at the crowded
      heaven,
And I said to my spirit, When we become the enfolders of those
      orbs and the pleasure and knowledge of every thing in them,
      shall we be filled and satisfied then?
And my spirit said No, we level that lift to pass and continue
      beyond.
1220 You are also asking me questions, and I hear you;
I answer that I cannot answer . . . . you must find out for yourself.

Sit awhile wayfarer,
Here are biscuits to eat and here is milk to drink,
But as soon as you sleep and renew yourself in sweet clothes I will
      certainly kiss you with my goodbye kiss and open the gate for
      your egress hence.

1225 Long enough have you dreamed contemptible dreams,
Now I wash the gum from your eyes,
You must habit yourself to the dazzle of the light and of every
      moment of your life.

Long have you timidly waded, holding a plank by the shore,
Now I will you to be a bold swimmer,
1230 To jump off in the midst of the sea, and rise again and nod to me
and shout, and laughingly dash with your hair.

[47]   I am the teacher of athletes,
He that by me spreads a wider breast than my own proves the
width of my own,
He most honors my style who learns under it to destroy the
teacher.

The boy I love, the same becomes a man not through derived
power but in his own right,
1235 Wicked, rather than virtuous out of conformity or fear,
Fond of his sweetheart, relishing well his steak,
Unrequited love or a slight cutting him worse than a wound cuts,
First rate to ride, to fight, to hit the bull's eye, to sail a skiff, to
sing a song or play on the banjo,
Preferring scars and faces pitted with smallpox over all latherers
and those that keep out of the sun.

1240 I teach straying from me, yet who can stray from me?
I follow you whoever you are from the present hour;
My words itch at your ears till you understand them.
I do not say these things for a dollar, or to fill up the time while I
wait for a boat;
It is you talking just as much myself . . . . I act as the tongue of
you,
1245 It was tied in your mouth . . . . in mine it begins to be loosened.

I swear I will never mention love or death inside a house,
And I swear I never will translate myself at all, only to him or her
who privately stays with me in the open air.

If you would understand me go to the heights or water-shore,
The nearest gnat is an explanation and a drop or the motion of
waves a key,
1250 The maul the oar and the handsaw second my words.

No shuttered room or school can commune with me,
But roughs and little children better than they.

The young mechanic is closest to me . . . . he knows me pretty
well,
The woodman that takes his axe and jug with him shall take me
with him all day,
1255 The farmboy ploughing in the field feels good at the sound of my
voice,

In vessels that sail my words must sail . . . . I go with fishermen
  and seamen, and love them,
My face rubs to the hunter's face when he lies down alone in his
  blanket,
The driver thinking of me does not mind the jolt of his wagon,
The young mother and old mother shall comprehend me,
1260 The girl and the wife rest the needle a moment and forget where
  they are,
They and all would resume what I have told them.

[48]   I have said that the soul is not more than the body,
And I have said that the body is not more than the soul,
And nothing, not God, is greater to one than one's-self is,
1265 And whoever walks a furlong without sympathy walks to his own
  funeral, dressed in his shroud,
And I or you pocketless of a dime may purchase the pick of the
  earth,
And to glance with an eye or show a bean in its pod confounds
  the learning of all times,
And there is no trade or employment but the young man following
  it may become a hero,
And there is no object so soft but it makes a hub for the wheeled
  universe,
1270 And any man or woman shall stand cool and supercilious before a
  million universes.

And I call to mankind, Be not curious about God,
For I who am curious about each am not curious about God,
No array of terms can say how much I am at peace about God
  and about death.

I hear and behold God in every object, yet I understand God not
  in the least,
1275 Nor do I understand who there can be more wonderful than
  myself.

Why should I wish to see God better than this day?
I see something of God each hour of the twenty-four, and each
  moment then,
In the faces of men and women I see God, and in my own face in
  the glass;
I find letters from God dropped in the street, and every one is
  signed by God's name,
1280 And I leave them where they are, for I know that others will
  punctually come forever and ever.

[49]   And as to you death, and you bitter hug of mortality . . . . it is
  idle to try to alarm me.

To his work without flinching the accoucheur[39] comes,
I see the elderhand pressing receiving supporting,
I recline by the sills of the exquisite flexible doors . . . . and mark
    the outlet, and mark the relief and escape.
1285 And as to you corpse I think you are good manure, but that does
    not offend me,
I smell the white roses sweetscented and growing,
I reach to the leafy lips . . . . I reach to the polished breasts of
    melons.

And as to you life, I reckon you are the leavings of many deaths,
No doubt I have died myself ten thousand times before.

1290 I hear you whispering there O stars of heaven,
O suns . . . . O grass of graves . . . . O perpetual transfers and
    promotions . . . . if you do not say anything how can I say
    anything?

Of the turbid pool that lies in the autumn forest,
Of the moon that descends the steeps of the soughing twilight,
Toss, sparkles of day and dusk . . . . toss on the black stems that
    decay in the muck,
1295 Toss to the moaning gibberish of the dry limbs.

I ascend from the moon . . . . I ascend from the night,
And perceive of the ghastly glitter the sunbeams reflected,
And debouch[40] to the steady and central from the offspring great
    or small.

[50]   There is that in me . . . . I do not know what it is . . . . but I
    know it is in me.

1300 Wrenched and sweaty . . . . calm and cool then my body becomes;
I sleep . . . . I sleep long.

I do not know it . . . . it is without name . . . . it is a word
    unsaid,
It is not in any dictionary or utterance or symbol.

Something it swings on more than the earth I swing on,
1305 To it the creation is the friend whose embracing awakes me.
Perhaps I might tell more . . . . Outlines! I plead for my brothers
    and sisters.

---

[39]French for midwife.
[40]From the French word *deboucher*, to issue
forth.

Do you see O my brothers and sisters?
It is not chaos or death . . . . it is form and union and plan . . . .
      it is eternal life . . . . it is happiness.

[51]   The past and present wilt . . . . I have filled them and emptied
            them,
1310 And proceed to fill my next fold of the future.

Listener up there! Here you . . . . what have you to confide to
      me?
Look in my face while I snuff the sidle of evening,
Talk honestly, for no one else hears you, and I stay only a minute
      longer.

Do I contradict myself?
1315 Very well then . . . . I contradict myself;
I am large . . . . I contain multitudes.

I concentrate toward them that are nigh . . . . I wait on the door-
      slab.

Who has done his day's work and will soonest be through with his
      supper?
Who wishes to walk with me?

1320 Will you speak before I am gone? Will you prove already too late?

[52]   The spotted hawk swoops by and accuses me . . . . he complains
            of my gab and my loitering.

I too am not a bit tamed . . . . I too am untranslatable,

I sound my barbaric yawp over the roofs of the world.
The last scud of day holds back for me,
1325 It flings my likeness after the rest and true as any on the shadowed
      wilds,
It coaxes me to the vapor and the dusk.

I depart as air . . . . I shake my white locks at the runaway sun,
I effuse my flesh in eddies and drift it in lacy jags.

I bequeath myself to the dirt to grow from the grass I love,
1330 If you want me again look for me under your bootsoles.

You will hardly know who I am or what I mean,
But I shall be good health to you nevertheless,
And filter and fibre your blood.

Failing to fetch me at first keep encouraged,
1335 Missing me one place search another,
I stop some where waiting for you[41]

1855

The Sleepers

[1] I wander all night in my vision,
Stepping with light feet . . . . swiftly and noiselessly stepping and
      stopping,
Bending with open eyes over the shut eyes of sleepers;
Wandering and confused . . . . lost to myself . . . . ill-assorted
      . . . . contradictory,
5 Pausing and gazing and bending and stopping.

How solemn they look there, stretched and still;
How quiet they breathe, the little children in their cradles.

The wretched features of ennuyees, the white features of corpses,
      the livid faces of drunkards, the sick-gray faces of onanists,[1]
The gashed bodies on battlefields, the insane in their strong-
      doored rooms, the sacred idiots,
10 The newborn emerging from gates and the dying emerging from
      gates,
The night pervades them and enfolds them.

The married couple sleep calmly in their bed, he with his palm on
      the hip of the wife, and she with her palm on the hip of the
      husband,
The sisters sleep lovingly side by side in their bed,
The men sleep lovingly side by side in theirs,
15 And the mother sleeps with her little child carefully wrapped.

The blind sleep, and the deaf and dumb sleep,
The prisoner sleeps well in the prison . . . . the runaway son
      sleeps,
The murderer that is to be hung next day . . . . how does he
      sleep?
And the murdered person . . . . how does he sleep?
20 The female that loves unrequited sleeps,
And the male that loves unrequited sleeps;

---

[41]There is no period at the end of the original
   version of "Song of Myself."

[1]Ennuyees, French for bored people; onanists,
   persons who masturbate.

The head of the moneymaker that plotted all day sleeps,
And the enraged and treacherous dispositions sleep.

I stand with drooping eyes by the worstsuffering and restless,
25 I pass my hands soothingly to and fro a few inches from them;
The restless sink in their beds . . . . they fitfully sleep.

The earth recedes from me into the night,
I saw that it was beautiful . . . . and I see that what is not the
      earth is beautiful.

I go from bedside to bedside . . . . I sleep close with the other
      sleepers, each in turn;
30 I dream in my dream all the dreams of the other dreamers,
And I become the other dreamers.

I am a dance . . . . Play up there! the fit is whirling me fast.

I am the everlaughing . . . . it is new moon and twilight,
I see the hiding of douceurs[2] . . . . I see nimble ghosts whichever
      way I look,
35 Cache and cache[3] again deep in the ground and sea, and where it
      is neither ground or sea.

Well do they do their jobs, those journeymen divine,
Only from me can they hide nothing and would not if they
      could;
I reckon I am their boss, and they make me a pet besides,
And surround me, and lead me and run ahead when I walk,
40 And lift their cunning covers and signify me with stretched arms,
      and resume the way;
Onward we move, a gay gang of blackguards with mirthshouting
      music and wildflapping pennants of joy.

I am the actor and the actress . . . . the voter . . the politician,
The emigrant and the exile . . the criminal that stood in the box,
He who has been famous, and he who shall be famous after today,
45 The stammerer . . . . the wellformed person . . the wasted or
      feeble person.

I am she who adorned herself and folded her hair expectantly,
My truant lover has come and it is dark.

---

[2]French for sweetness, delight, pleasure.
[3]French for hide.

Double yourself and receive me darkness,
Receive me and my lover too . . . . he will not let me go without him.

50 I roll myself upon you as upon a bed . . . . I resign myself to the
   dusk.

He whom I call answers me and takes the place of my lover,
He rises with me silently from the bed.

Darkness you are gentler than my lover . . . . his flesh was sweaty
   and panting,
I feel the hot moisture yet that he left me.

55 My hands are spread forth . . I pass them in all directions,
I would sound up the shadowy shore to which you are journeying.

Be careful, darkness . . . . already, what was it touched me?
I thought my lover had gone . . . . else darkness and he are one,
I hear the heart-beat . . . . I follow . . I fade away.

60 O hotcheeked and blushing! O foolish hectic!
O for pity's sake, no one must see me now! . . . . my clothes were
   stolen while I was abed,
Now I am thrust forth, where shall I run?

Pier that I saw dimly last night when I looked from the windows,
Pier out from the main, let me catch myself with you and stay
   . . . . I will not chafe you;
65 I feel ashamed to go naked about the world,
And am curious to know where my feet stand . . . . and what is
   this flooding me, childhood or manhood . . . . and the hunger
   that crosses the bridge between.

The cloth laps a first sweet eating and drinking,
Laps life-swelling yolks . . . . laps ear of rose-corn, milky and just
   ripened:
The white teeth stay, and the boss-tooth advances in darkness,
70 And liquor is spilled on lips and bosoms by touching glasses, and
   the best liquor afterward.

[2]   I descend my western course . . . . my sinews are flaccid,
         Perfume and youth course through me, and I am their wake.

It is my face yellow and wrinkled instead of the old woman's,
I sit low in a strawbottom chair and carefully darn my grandson's
   stockings.

75 It is I too . . . . the sleepless widow looking out on the winter
      midnight,
    I see the sparkles of starshine on the icy and pallid earth.

    A shroud I see—and I am the shroud . . . . I wrap a body and lie
      in the coffin;
    It is dark here underground . . . . it is not evil or pain here . . . .
      it is blank here, for reasons.

    It seems to me that everything in the light and air ought to be
      happy;
80 Whoever is not in his coffin and the dark grave, let him know he
      has enough.

[3]   I see a beautiful gigantic swimmer swimming naked through the
          eddies of the sea,
        His brown hair lies close and even to his head . . . . he strikes out
          with courageous arms . . . . he urges himself with his legs.
        I see his white body . . . . I see his undaunted eyes;
        I hate the swift-running eddies that would dash him headforemost
          on the rocks.

85   What are you doing you ruffianly red-trickled waves?
        Will you kill the courageous giant? Will you kill him in the prime
          of his middle age?

        Steady and long he struggles;
        He is baffled and banged and bruised . . . . he holds out while his
          strength holds out,
        The slapping eddies are spotted with his blood . . . . they bear
          him away . . . . they roll him and swing him and turn him:
90   His beautiful body is borne in the circling eddies . . . . it is
          continually bruised on rocks,
        Swiftly and out of sight is borne the brave corpse.

[4]   I turn but do not extricate myself;
        Confused . . . . a pastreading . . . . another, but with darkness yet.

        The beach is cut by the razory ice-wind . . . . the wreck-guns
          sound,
95   The tempest lulls and the moon comes floundering through the
          drifts.

        I look where the ship helplessly heads end on . . . . I hear the
          burst as she strikes . . . . I hear the howls of dismay . . . .
          they grow fainter and fainter.

I cannot aid with my wringing fingers;
I can but rush to the surf and let it drench me and freeze upon
    me.

I search with the crowd . . . . not one of the company is washed
    to us alive;
100 In the morning I help pick up the dead and lay them in rows in a
    barn.

[5]   Now of the old war-days . . the defeat at Brooklyn;[4]
Washington stands inside the lines . . he stands on the
    entrenched hills amid a crowd of officers,
His face is cold and damp . . . . he cannot repress the weeping
    drops . . . . he lifts the glass perpetually to his eyes . . . . the
    color is blanched from his cheeks,
He sees the slaughter of the southern braves confided to him by
    their parents.

105 The same at last and at last when peace is declared,[5]
He stands in the room of the old tavern . . . . the wellbeloved
    soldiers all pass through,
The officers speechless and slow draw near in their turns,
The chief encircles their necks with his arm and kisses them on the
    cheek,
He kisses lightly the wet cheeks one after another . . . . he shakes
    hands and bids goodbye to the army.

[6]   110 Now I tell what my mother told me today as we sat at dinner
    together,
Of when she was a nearly grown girl living home with her parents
    on the old homestead.

A red squaw came one breakfasttime to the old homestead,
On her back she carried a bundle of rushes for rushbottoming
    chairs;
Her hair straight shiny coarse black and profuse halfenveloped her
    face,
115 Her step was free and elastic . . . . her voice sounded exquisitely
    as she spoke.

My mother looked in delight and amazement at the stranger,
She looked at the beauty of her tallborne face and full and pliant
    limbs,
The more she looked upon her she loved her,

---

[4]Whitman describes Washington's reaction to the American defeat at the Battle of Brooklyn Heights at the outset of the Revolutionary War.

[5]Washington bid farewell to his troops in 1783 at Fraunce's Tavern in New York City.

Never before had she seen such wonderful beauty and purity;
120 She made her sit on a bench by the jamb of the fireplace . . . . she
    cooked food for her,
She had no work to give her but she gave her remembrance and
    fondness.

The red squaw staid all the forenoon, and toward the middle of
    the afternoon she went away;
O my mother was loth to have her go away,
All the week she thought of her . . . . she watched for her many a
    month,
125 She remembered her many a winter and many a summer,
But the red squaw never came nor was heard of there again.

Now Lucifer was not dead . . . . or if he was I am his sorrowful
    terrible heir;[6]
I have been wronged . . . . I am oppressed . . . . I hate him that
    oppresses me,
I will either destroy him, or he shall release me.

130 Damn him! how he does defile me,
How he informs against my brother and sister and takes pay for
    their blood,
How he laughs when I look down the bend after the steamboat
    that carries away my woman.

Now the vast dusk bulk that is the whale's bulk . . . . it seems
    mine,
Warily, sportsman! though I lie so sleepy and sluggish, my tap is
    death.

[7]   135 A show of the summer softness . . . . a contact of something
    unseen . . . . an amour of the light and air;
I am jealous and overwhelmed with friendliness,
And will go gallivant with the light and the air myself,
And have an unseen something to be in contact with them also.

O love and summer! you are in the dreams and in me,
140 Autumn and winter are in the dreams . . . . the farmer goes with
    his thrift,
The droves and crops increase . . . . the barns are wellfilled.
Elements merge in the night . . . . ships make tacks in the dreams
    . . . . the sailor sails . . . . the exile returns home,
The fugitive returns unharmed . . . . the immigrant is back beyond
    months and years;

[6]A slave is speaking these words.

The poor Irishman lives in the simple house of his childhood, with
    the wellknown neighbors and faces,
145 They warmly welcome him . . . . he is barefoot again . . . . he
    forgets he is welloff;
The Dutchman voyages home, and the Scotchman and Welchman
    voyage home . . . . and the native of the Mediterranean
    voyages home;
To every port of England and France and Spain enter wellfilled
    ships;
The Swiss foots it toward his hills . . . . the Prussian goes his way,
    and the Hungarian his way, and the Pole goes his way,
The Swede returns, and the Dane and Norwegian return.

150 The homeward bound and the outward bound,
The beautiful lost swimmer, the ennuyee, the onanist, the female
    that loves unrequited, the moneymaker,
The actor and actress . . those through with their parts and
    those waiting to commence,
The affectionate boy, the husband and wife, the voter, the nominee
    that is chosen and the nominee that has failed,
The great already known, and the great anytime after to day,
155 The stammerer, the sick, the perfectformed, the homely,
The criminal that stood in the box, the judge that sat and
    sentenced him, the fluent lawyers, the jury, the audience,
The laugher and weeper, the dancer, the midnight widow, the red
    squaw,
The consumptive, the erysipalite,[7] the idiot, he that is wronged,
The antipodes, and every one between this and them in the dark,
160 I swear they are averaged now . . . . one is no better than the
    other,
The night and sleep have likened them and restored them.
I swear they are all beautiful,
Every one that sleeps is beautiful . . . . every thing in the dim
    night is beautiful,
The wildest and bloodiest is over and all is peace.

165 Peace is always beautiful,
The myth of heaven indicates peace and night.

The myth of heaven indicates the soul;
The soul is always beautiful . . . . it appears more or it appears
    less . . . . it comes or lags behind,
It comes from its embowered garden and looks pleasantly on itself
    and encloses the world;

---

[7]Someone suffering from erysipelas, a skin disease.

170 Perfect and clean the genitals previously jetting, and perfect and
      clean the womb cohering,
The head wellgrown and proportioned and plumb, and the bowels
      and joints proportioned and plumb.

The soul is always beautiful,
The universe is duly in order . . . . every thing is in its place,
What is arrived is in its place, and what waits is in its place;
175 The twisted skull waits . . . . the watery or rotten blood waits,
The child of the glutton or venerealee waits long, and the child of
      the drunkard waits long, and the drunkard himself waits long,
The sleepers that lived and died wait . . . . the far advanced are to
      go on in their turns, and the far behind are to go on in their
      turns,
The diverse shall be no less diverse, but they shall flow and unite
      . . . . they unite now.

The sleepers are very beautiful as they lie unclothed,
180 They flow hand in hand over the whole earth from east to west as
      they lie unclothed;
The Asiatic and African are hand in hand . . . . the European and
      American are hand in hand,
Learned and unlearned are hand in hand . . and male and
      female are hand in hand;
The bare arm of the girl crosses the bare breast of her lover . . . .
      they press close without lust . . . . his lips press her neck,
The father holds his grown or ungrown son in his arms with
      measureless love . . . . and the son holds the father in his
      arms with measureless love,
185 The white hair of the mother shines on the white wrist of the
      daughter,
The breath of the boy goes with the breath of the man . . . .
      friend is inarmed by friend,
The scholar kisses the teacher and the teacher kisses the scholar
      . . . . the wronged is made right,
The call of the slave is one with the master's call . . . . and the
      master salutes the slave,
The felon steps forth from the prison . . . . the insane becomes
      sane . . . . the suffering of sick persons is relieved,
190 The sweatings and fevers stop . . the throat that was unsound is
      sound . . the lungs of the consumptive are resumed . .
      the poor distressed head is free,
The joints of the rheumatic move as smoothly as ever, and
      smoother than ever,
Stiflings and passages open . . . . the paralysed become supple,
The swelled and convulsed and congested awake to themselves in
      condition,

They pass the invigoration of the night and the chemistry of the
    night and awake.

195 I too pass from the night;
    I stay awhile away O night, but I return to you again and love
        you;
    Why should I be afraid to trust myself to you?
    I am not afraid . . . . I have been well brought forward by you;
    I love the rich running day, but I do not desert her in whom I lay
        so long;
200 I know not how I came of you, and I know not where I go with
        you . . . . but I know I came well and shall go well.
    I will stop only a time with the night . . . . and rise betimes.

I will duly pass the day O my mother and duly return to you;
Not you will yield forth the dawn again more surely than you will
    yield forth me again,
Not the womb yields the babe in its time more surely than I shall
    be yielded from you in my time.

1855

Inscriptions[1]

One's-Self I Sing

One's-Self I sing, a simple separate person,
Yet utter the word Democratic, the word En-Masse.

Of physiology from top to toe I sing,
Not physiognomy alone nor brain alone is worthy for the Muse, I
    say the Form complete is worthier far,
5 The Female equally with the Male I sing.

Of Life immense in passion, pulse, and power,
Cheerful, for freest action form'd under the laws divine,
The Modern Man I sing.

1867

---

[1]*Inscriptions* first appeared as the opening grouping in the 1871 edition of *Leaves of Grass*. Beginning in 1867, "One's-Self I Sing" appeared as the opening poem of all future editions of *Leaves of Grass*.

Children of Adam[1]

To the Garden the World

To the garden the world anew ascending,
Potent mates, daughters, sons, preluding,
The love, the life of their bodies, meaning and being,
Curious here behold my resurrection after slumber,
5 The revolving cycles in their wide sweep having brought me again,
Amorous, mature, all beautiful to me, all wondrous,
My limbs and the quivering fire that ever plays through them, for
    reasons, most wondrous,
Existing I peer and penetrate still,
Content with the present, content with the past,
10 By my side or back of me Eve following,
Or in front, and I following her just the same.

                                      1860

A Woman Waits for Me

A woman waits for me, she contains all, nothing is lacking,
Yet all were lacking if sex were lacking, or if the moisture of the
    right man were lacking.

Sex contains all, bodies, souls,
Meanings, proofs, purities, delicacies, results, promulgations
5 Songs, commands, health, pride, the maternal mystery, the seminal
    milk,
All hopes, benefactions, bestowals, all the passions, loves, beauties,
    delights of the earth,
All the governments, judges, gods, follow'd persons of the earth,
These are contain'd in sex as parts of itself and justifications of
    itself.

Without shame the man I like knows and avows the deliciousness
    of his sex,
10 Without shame the woman I like knows and avows hers.

---

[1]*Children of Adam* and its companion cluster *Calamus,* which first appeared in the 1860 edition of *Leaves of Grass,* are Whitman's most controversial poetic sequences. In *Children of Adam* he focuses on what he calls "amative love," the phrenological term for the love between men and women. In *Calamus* he focuses on "adhesive love," the phrenological term for the love between men.

Now I will dismiss myself from impassive women,
I will go stay with her who waits for me, and with those women
    that are warm-blooded and sufficient for me,
I see that they understand me and do not deny me,
I see that they are worthy of me, I will be the robust husband of
    those women.

15 They are not one jot less than I am,
They are tann'd in the face by shining suns and blowing winds,
Their flesh has the old divine suppleness and strength,
They know how to swim, row, ride, wrestle, shoot, run, strike,
    retreat, advance, resist, defend themselves,
They are ultimate in their own right—they are calm, clear, well-
    possess'd of themselves.

20 I draw you close to me, you women,
I cannot let you go, I would do you good,
I am for you, and you are for me, not only for our own sake, but
    for others' sakes,
Envelop'd in you sleep greater heroes and bards,
They refuse to awake at the touch of any man but me.

25 It is I, you women, I make my way,
I am stern, acrid, large, undissuadable, but I love you,
I do not hurt you any more than is necessary for you,
I pour the stuff to start sons and daughters fit for these States, I
    press with slow rude muscle,
I brace myself effectually, I listen to no entreaties,
30 I dare not withdraw till I deposit what has so long accumulated
    within me.

Through you I drain the pent-up rivers of myself,
In you I wrap a thousand onward years,
On you I graft the grafts of the best-beloved of me and America,
The drops I distil upon you shall grow fierce and athletic girls,
    new artists, musicians, and singers,
35 The babes I beget upon you are to beget babes in their turn,
I shall demand perfect men and women out of my love-spendings,
I shall expect them to interpenetrate with others, as I and you
    interpenetrate now,
I shall count on the fruits of the gushing showers of them, as I
    count on the fruits of the gushing showers I give now,
I shall look for loving crops from the birth, life, death,
    immortality, I plant so lovingly now.

1856

Calamus[1]

In Paths Untrodden

In paths untrodden,
In the growth by margins of pond-waters,
Escaped from the life that exhibits itself,
From all the standards hitherto publish'd, from the pleasures,
    profits, conformities,
5 Which too long I was offering to feed my soul,
Clear to me now standards not yet publish'd, clear to me that my
    soul,
That the soul of the man I speak for rejoices in comrades,
Here by myself away from the clank of the world,
Tallying and talk'd to here by tongues aromatic,
10 No longer abash'd, (for in this secluded spot I can respond as I
    would not dare elsewhere,)
Strong upon me the life that does not exhibit itself, yet contains all
    the rest,
Resolv'd to sing no songs to-day but those of manly attachment,
Projecting them along that substantial life,
Bequeathing hence types of athletic love,
15 Afternoon this delicious Ninth-month[2] in my forty-first year,
I proceed for all who are or have been young men,
To tell the secret of my nights and days,
To celebrate the need of comrades.

                             1860

Recorders Ages Hence

Recorders ages hence,
Come, I will take you down underneath this impassive exterior, I
    will tell you what to say of me,
Publish my name and hang up my picture as that of the tenderest
    lover,
The friend the lover's portrait, of whom his friend his lover was
    fondest,

---

[1]Calamus is another word for sweet flag, a hardy, aromatic grass that grows near ponds and swamps.

[2]Quaker term for September, the 9th month of the year. Whitman associated the pagan names of the days and the months with the feudal past; his substitution of Quaker names was part of his attempt to invent a specifically American idiom expressive of the beliefs and values of the American people.

5 Who was not proud of his songs, but of the measureless ocean of
    love within him, and freely pour'd it forth,
Who often walk'd lonesome walks thinking of his dear friends, his
    lovers,
Who pensive away from one he lov'd often lay sleepless and
    dissatisfied at night,
Who knew too well the sick, sick dread lest the one he lov'd
    might secretly be indifferent to him,
Whose happiest days were far away through fields, in woods, on
    hills, he and another wandering hand in hand, they twain
    apart from other men,
10 Who oft as he saunter'd the streets curv'd with his arm the
    shoulder of his friend, while the arm of his friend rested upon
    him also.

1860

When I Heard at the Close of the Day

When I heard at the close of the day how my name had been
    receiv'd with plaudits in the capitol, still it was not a happy
    night for me that follow'd,
And else when I carous'd, or when my plans were accomplish'd,
    still I was not happy,
But the day when I rose at dawn from the bed of perfect health,
    refresh'd, singing, inhaling the ripe breath of autumn,
When I saw the full moon in the west grow pale and disappear in
    the morning light,
5 When I wander'd alone over the beach, and undressing bathed,
    laughing with the cool waters, and saw the sun rise,
And when I thought how my dear friend my lover was on his way
    coming, O then I was happy,
O then each breath tasted sweeter, and all that day my food
    nourish'd me more, and the beautiful day pass'd well,
And the next came with equal joy, and with the next at evening
    came my friend,
And that night while all was still I heard the waters roll slowly
    continually up the shores,
10 I heard the hissing rustle of the liquid and sands as directed to me
    whispering to congratulate me,
For the one I love most lay sleeping by me under the same cover
    in the cool night,
In the stillness in the autumn moonbeams his face was inclined
    toward me,
And his arm lay lightly around my breast—and that night I was
    happy.

1860

Here the Frailest Leaves of Me

Here the frailest leaves of me and yet my strongest lasting,
Here I shade and hide my thoughts, I myself do not expose them,
And yet they expose me more than all my other poems.

1860

I Dream'd in a Dream

I dream'd in a dream I saw a city invincible to the attacks of the
    whole of the rest of the earth,
I dream'd that was the new city of Friends,
Nothing was greater there than the quality of robust love, it led
    the rest,
It was seen every hour in the actions of the men of that city,
5 And in all their looks and words.

1860

Sea-Drift

Out of the Cradle Endlessly Rocking

Out of the cradle endlessly rocking,
Out of the mocking-bird's throat, the musical shuttle,
Out of the Ninth-month midnight,
Over the sterile sands and the fields beyond, where the child
    leaving his bed wander'd alone, bareheaded, barefoot,
5 Down from the shower'd halo,
Up from the mystic play of shadows twining and twisting as if they
    were alive,
Out from the patches of briers and blackberries,
From the memories of the bird that chanted to me,
From your memories sad brother, from the fitful risings and
    fallings I heard,
10 From under that yellow half-moon late-risen and swollen as if with
    tears,
From those beginning notes of yearning and love there in the mist,
From the thousand responses of my heart never to cease,
From the myriad thence-arous'd words,
From the word stronger and more delicious than any,

15 From such as now they start the scene revisiting,
      As a flock, twittering, rising, or overhead passing,
      Borne hither, ere all eludes me, hurriedly,
      A man, yet by these tears a little boy again,
      Throwing myself on the sand, confronting the waves,
20 I, chanter of pains and joys, uniter of here and hereafter,
      Taking all hints to use them, but swiftly leaping beyond them,
      A reminiscence sing.
      Once Paumanok,[1]
      When the lilac-scent was in the air and Fifth-month grass was
            growing,
25 Up this seashore in some briers,
      Two feather'd guests from Alabama, two together,
      And their nest, and four light-green eggs spotted with brown.
      And every day the he-bird to and fro near at hand.
      And every day the she-bird crouch'd on her nest, silent, with
            bright eyes,
30 And every day I, a curious boy, never too close, never disturbing
            them,
      Cautiously peering, absorbing, translating.

      Shine! shine! shine!
      Pour down your warmth, great sun!
      While we bask, we two together.

35 *Two together!*
      Winds blow south, or winds blow north,
      Day come white, or night come black,
      Home, or rivers and mountains from home,
      Singing all time, minding no time,
40 *While we two keep together.*

      Till of a sudden,
      May-be kill'd, unknown to her mate,
      One forenoon the she-bird crouch'd not on the nest,
      Nor return'd that afternoon, nor the next,
45 Nor ever appear'd again.

      And thenceforward all summer in the sound of the sea,
      And at night under the full of the moon in calmer weather,
      Over the hoarse surging of the sea,
      Or flitting from brier to brier by day,
50 I saw, I heard at intervals the remaining one, the he-bird,
      The solitary guest from Alabama.

[1]Native American Indian name for Long
Island.

Blow! blow! blow!
Blow up sea-winds along Paumanok's shore;
I wait and I wait till you blow my mate to me.

55 Yes, when the stars glisten'd,
    All night long on the prong of a moss-scallop'd stake,
    Down almost amid the slapping waves,
    Sat the lone singer wonderful causing tears.

    He call'd on his mate,
60 He pour'd forth the meanings which I of all men know.

    Yes my brother I know,
    The rest might not, but I have treasur'd every note,
    For more than once dimly down to the beach gliding,
    Silent, avoiding the moonbeams, blending myself with the shadows,
65 Recalling now the obscure shapes, the echoes, the sounds and
        sights after their sorts,
    The white arms out in the breakers tirelessly tossing,
    I, with bare feet, a child, the wind wafting my hair,
    Listen'd long and long.

    Listen'd to keep, to sing, now translating the notes,
70 Following you my brother.

Soothe! soothe! soothe!
Close on its wave soothes the wave behind,
And again another behind embracing and lapping, every one
    close,
But my love soothes not me, not me.

75 *Low hangs the moon, it rose late,*
    It is lagging—O I think it is heavy with love, with love.

    O madly the sea pushes upon the land,
    With love, with love.

    O night! do I not see my love fluttering out among the breakers?
80 *What is that little black thing I see there in the white?*

    Loud! loud! loud!
    Loud I call to you, my love!

    High and clear I shoot my voice over the waves,
    Surely you must know who is here, is here,
85 *You must know who I am, my love.*

Low-hanging moon!
What is that dusky spot in your brown yellow?
O it is the shape, the shape of my mate!
O moon do not keep her from me any longer.

90 *Land! land! O land!*
Whichever way I turn, O I think you could give me my mate back
again if you only would,
For I am almost sure I see her dimly whichever way I look.

O rising stars!
Perhaps the one I want so much will rise, will rise with some of you.

95 *O throat! O trembling throat!*
Sound clearer through the atmosphere!
Pierce the woods, the earth,
Somewhere listening to catch you must be the one I want.

Shake out carols!
100 *Solitary here, the night's carols!*
Carols of lonesome love! death's carols!
Carols under that lagging, yellow, waning moon!
O under that moon where she droops almost down into the sea!
O reckless despairing carols.

105 *But soft! sink low!*
Soft! let me just murmur,
And do you wait a moment you husky-nois'd sea,
For somewhere I believe I heard my mate responding to me,
So faint, I must be still, be still to listen,
110 *But not altogether still, for then she might not come immediately to*
me.

Hither my love!
Here I am! here!
With this just-sustain'd note I announce myself to you,
This gentle call is for you my love, for you.

115 *Do not be decoy'd elsewhere,*
That is the whistle of the wind, it is not my voice,
That is the fluttering, the fluttering of the spray,
Those are the shadows of leaves.

O darkness! O in vain!
120 *O I am very sick and sorrowful.*

O brown halo in the sky near the moon, drooping upon the sea!
O troubled reflection in the sea!
O throat! O throbbing heart!
And I singing uselessly, uselessly all the night.

125 *O past! O happy life! O songs of joy!*
In the air, in the woods, over fields,

Loved! loved! loved! loved! loved!
But my mate no more, no more with me!
We two together no more.

130 The aria sinking,
All else continuing, the stars shining,
The winds blowing, the notes of the bird continuous echoing,
With angry moans the fierce old mother incessantly moaning,
On the sands of Paumanok's shore gray and rustling,
135 The yellow half-moon enlarged, sagging down, drooping, the face
        of the sea almost touching,
The boy ecstatic, with his bare feet the waves, with his hair the
        atmosphere dallying,
The love in the heart long pent, now loose, now at last
        tumultuously bursting,
The aria's meaning, the ears, the soul, swiftly depositing,
The strange tears down the cheeks coursing,
140 The colloquy there, the trio, each uttering,
The undertone, the savage old mother incessantly crying,
To the boy's soul's questions sullenly timing, some drown'd secret
        hissing,
To the outsetting bard.

Demon or bird! (said the boy's soul,)
145 Is it indeed toward your mate you sing? or is it really to me?
For I, that was a child, my tongue's use sleeping, now I have
        heard you,
Now in a moment I know what I am for, I awake,
And already a thousand singers, a thousand songs, clearer, louder
        and more sorrowful than yours,
A thousand warbling echoes have started to life within me, never
        to die.
150 O you singer solitary, singing by yourself, projecting me,
O solitary me listening, never more shall I cease perpetuating you,
Never more shall I escape, never more the reverberations,
Never more the cries of unsatisfied love be absent from me,
Never again leave me to be the peaceful child I was before what
        there in the night,

155 By the sea under the yellow and sagging moon,
The messenger there arous'd, the fire, the sweet hell within,
The unknown want, the destiny of me.

O give me the clew! (it lurks in the night here somewhere,)
O if I am to have so much, let me have more!

160 A word then, (for I will conquer it,)
The word final, superior to all,
Subtle, sent up—what is it?—I listen;
Are you whispering it, and have been all the time, you sea-waves?
Is that it from your liquid rims and wet sands?

165 Whereto answering, the sea,
Delaying not, hurrying not,
Whisper'd me through the night, and very plainly before daybreak,
Lisp'd to me the low and delicious word death,
And again death, death, death, death,
170 Hissing melodious, neither like the bird nor like my arous'd child's
          heart,
But edging near as privately for me rustling at my feet,
Creeping thence steadily up to my ears and laving me softly all
          over,
Death, death, death, death, death.

Which I do not forget,
175 But fuse the song of my dusky demon and brother,
That he sang to me in the moonlight on Paumanok's gray beach,
With the thousand responsive songs at random,
My own songs awaked from that hour,
And with them the key, the word up from the waves,
180 The word of the sweetest song and all songs,
That strong and delicious word which, creeping to my feet,
(Or like some old crone rocking the cradle, swathed in sweet
          garments, bending aside,)
The sea whisper'd me.

                                                                    1859

By the Roadside

Europe[1]
The 72d and 73d Years of These States

Suddenly out of its stale and drowsy lair, the lair of slaves,
Like lightning it le'pt forth half startled at itself,
Its feet upon the ashes and the rags, its hands tight to the throats
    of kings.

O hope and faith!
5 O aching close of exiled patriots' lives!
O many a sicken'd heart!
Turn back unto this day and make yourselves afresh.

And you, paid to defile the People—you liars, mark!
Not for numberless agonies, murders, lusts,
10 For court thieving in its manifold mean forms, worming from his
    simplicity the poor man's wages,
For many a promise sworn by royal lips and broken and laugh'd at
    in the breaking,
Then in their power not for all these did the blows strike revenge,
    or the heads of the nobles fall;
The People scorn'd the ferocity of kings.

But the sweetness of mercy brew'd bitter destruction, and the
    frighten'd monarchs come back,
15 Each comes in state with his train, hangman, priest, tax-gatherer,
Soldier, lawyer, lord, jailer, and sycophant.

Yet behind all lowering stealing, lo, a shape,
Vague as the night, draped interminably, head, front and form, in
    scarlet folds,
Whose face and eyes none may see,
20 Out of its robes only this, the red robes lifted by the arm,
One finger crook'd pointed high over the top, like the head of a
    snake appears.

Meanwhile corpses lie in new-made graves, bloody corpses of
    young men,

---

[1]This poem, which was first published in the *New York Daily Tribune* on June 21, 1850, was included among the initial twelve poems of *Leaves of Grass* in 1855. It was inspired by the 1848 revolutions throughout Europe.

The rope of the gibbet hangs heavily, the bullets of princes are
     flying, the creatures of power laugh aloud,
And all these things bear fruits, and they are good.

25 Those corpses of young men,
     Those martyrs that hang from the gibbets, those hearts pierc'd by
     the gray lead,
     Cold and motionless as they seem live elsewhere with unslaughter'd
     vitality.

They live in other young men O kings!
They live in brothers again ready to defy you,
30 They were purified by death, they were taught and exalted.

Not a grave of the murder'd for freedom but grows seed for
     freedom, in its turn to bear seed,
Which the winds carry afar and re-sow, and the rains and the
     snows nourish.

Not a disembodied spirit can the weapons of tyrants let loose,
But it stalks invisibly over the earth, whispering, counseling,
     cautioning.

35 Liberty, let others despair of you—I never despair of you.

Is the house shut? is the master away?
Nevertheless, be ready, be not weary of watching,
He will soon return, his messengers come anon.

1850

When I Heard the Learn'd Astronomer

When I heard the learn'd astronomer,
When the proofs, the figures, were ranged in columns before me,
When I was shown the charts and diagrams, to add, divide, and
     measure them,
When I sitting heard the astronomer where he lectured with much
     applause in the lecture-room,
5 How soon unaccountable I became tired and sick,
Till rising and gliding out I wander'd off by myself,
In the mystical moist night-air, and from time to time,
Look'd up in perfect silence at the stars.

1865

To a President[1]

All you are doing and saying is to America dangled mirages,
You have not learn'd of Nature—of the politics of Nature you
      have not learn'd the great amplitude, rectitude, impartiality,
You have not seen that only such as they are for these States,
And that what is less than they must sooner or later lift off from
      these States.

                                       1860

The Dalliance of the Eagles

Skirting the river road, (my forenoon walk, my rest,)
Skyward in air a sudden muffled sound, the dalliance of the eagles,
The rushing amorous contact high in space together,
The clinching interlocking claws, a living, fierce, gyrating wheel,
5 Four beating wings, two beaks, a swirling mass tight grappling,
In tumbling turning clustering loops, straight downward falling,
Till o'er the river pois'd, the twain yet one, a moment's lull,
A motionless still balance in the air, then parting, talons loosing,
Upward again on slow-firm pinions slanting, their separate diverse
      flight,
10 She hers, he his, pursuing.

                                       1880

To the States

To Identify the 16th, 17th, or 18th Presidentiad.[1]

Why reclining, interrogating? why myself and all drowsing?
What deepening twilight—scum floating atop of the waters,
Who are they as bats and night-dogs askant in the capitol?
What a filthy Presidentiad! (O South, your torrid suns! O North,
      your arctic freezings!)

---

[1]The poem was initially addressed to James Buchanan, the Democratic president whose support for slavery expansion and other controversial policies seemed, in Whitman's view, to undermine the fundamental values of the American republic.

[1]The 16th, 17th, and 18th Presentiad refers to the presidencies of Millard Fillmore, Franklin Pierce, and James Buchanan, all of whom pursued a policy of compromise on the issue of slavery in order to avoid armed conflict between North and South. The poem, which was included in the 1860 edition of *Leaves of Grass,* appears to predict the imminent outbreak of the Civil War.

5   Are those really Congressmen? are those the great Judges?[2] is that
     the President?
   Then I will sleep awhile yet, for I see that these States sleep, for
     reasons;
   (With gathering murk, with muttering thunder and lambent shoots
     we all duly awake,
   South, North, East, West, inland and seaboard, we will surely
     awake.)

1860

Drum-Taps[1]

Beat! Beat! Drums!

Beat! beat! drums!—blow! bugles! blow!
Through the windows—through doors—burst like a ruthless force,
Into the solemn church, and scatter the congregation,
Into the school where the scholar is studying;
5   Leave not the bridegroom quiet—no happiness must he have now
     with his bride,
   Nor the peaceful farmer any peace, ploughing his field or
     gathering his grain,
   So fierce you whirr and pound you drums—so shrill you bugles
     blow.

Beat! beat! drums!—blow! bugles! blow!
Over the traffic of cities—over the rumble of wheels in the streets;
10 Are beds prepared for sleepers at night in the houses? no sleepers
     must sleep in those beds,
   No bargainers' bargains by day—no brokers or speculators—
     would they continue?
   Would the talkers be talking? would the singer attempt to sing?
   Would the lawyer rise in the court to state his case before the
     judge?
   Then rattle quicker, heavier drums—you bugles wilder blow.

15 Beat! beat! drums!—blow! bugles! blow!
   Make no parley—stop for no expostulation,

---

[2]Whitman may be referring to Chief Justice
Taney's 1857 Dred Scott Decision, which denied blacks citizenship under the Constitution
of the United States.

[1]*Drum-Taps* was initially published as a separate volume in 1865. It was added to *Leaves of
Grass* in 1867.

Mind not the timid—mind not the weeper or prayer,
Mind not the old man beseeching the young man,
Let not the child's voice be heard, nor the mother's entreaties,
20 Make even the trestles to shake the dead where they lie awaiting
    the hearses,
So strong you thump O terrible drums—so loud you bugles blow.

                                      1861

Cavalry Crossing a Ford

A line in long array where they wind betwixt green islands,
They take a serpentine course, their arms flash in the sun—hark to
    the musical clank,
Behold the silvery river, in it the splashing horses loitering stop to
    drink,
Behold the brown-faced men, each group, each person a picture,
    the negligent rest on the saddles,
5 Some emerge on the opposite bank, others are just entering the
    ford—while,
Scarlet and blue and snowy white,
The guidon flags flutter gayly in the wind.

                                        1865

Vigil Strange I Kept on the Field One Night

Vigil strange I kept on the field one night;
When you my son and my comrade dropt at my side that day,
One look I but gave which your dear eyes return'd with a look I
    shall never forget,
One touch of your hand to mine O boy, reach'd up as you lay on
    the ground,
5 Then onward I sped in the battle, the even-contested battle,
Till late in the night reliev'd to the place at last again I made my
    way,
Found you in death so cold dear comrade, found your body son of
    responding kisses, (never again on earth responding,)
Bared your face in the starlight, curious the scene, cool blew the
    moderate night-wind,
Long there and then in vigil I stood, dimly around me the battle-
    field spreading,
10 Vigil wondrous and vigil sweet there in the fragrant silent night,
But not a tear fell, not even a long-drawn sigh, long, long I gazed,
Then on the earth partially reclining sat by your side leaning my
    chin in my hands,

Passing sweet hours, immortal and mystic hours with you dearest
    comrade—not a tear, not a word,
Vigil of silence, love and death, vigil for you my son and my
    soldier,
15 As onward silently stars aloft, eastward new ones upward stole,
Vigil final for you brave boy, (I could not save you, swift was your
    death,
I faithfully loved you and cared for you living, I think we shall
    surely meet again,)
Till at latest lingering of the night, indeed just as the dawn
    appear'd,
My comrade I wrapt in his blanket, envelop'd well his form,
20 Folded the blanket well, tucking it carefully over head and
    carefully under feet,
And there and then and bathed by the rising sun, my son in his
    grave, in his rude-dug grave I deposited,
Ending my vigil strange with that, vigil of night and battle-field
    dim,
Vigil for boy of responding kisses, (never again on earth
    responding,)
Vigil for comrade swiftly slain, vigil I never forget, how as day
    brighten'd,
25 I rose from the chill ground and folded my soldier well in his
    blanket,
And buried him where he fell.

1865

A March in the Ranks Hard-Prest, and the Road Unknown

A march in the ranks hard-prest, and the road unknown,
A route through a heavy wood with muffled steps in the darkness,
Our army foil'd with loss severe, and the sullen remnant retreating,
Till after midnight glimmer upon us the lights of a dim-lighted
    building,
5 We come to an open space in the woods, and halt by the dim-
    lighted building,
'Tis a large old church at the crossing roads, now an impromptu
    hospital,
Entering but for a minute I see a sight beyond all the pictures and
    poems ever made,
Shadows of deepest, deepest black, just lit by moving candles and
    lamps,
And by one great pitchy torch stationary with wild red flame and
    clouds of smoke,

10   By these, crowds, groups of forms vaguely I see on the floor, some
      in the pews laid down,
    At my feet more distinctly a soldier, a mere lad, in danger of
      bleeding to death, (he is shot in the abdomen,)
    I stanch the blood temporarily, (the youngster's face is white as a
      lily,)
    Then before I depart I sweep my eyes o'er the scene fain to
      absorb it all,
    Faces, varieties, postures beyond description, most in obscurity,
      some of them dead,
15   Surgeons operating, attendants holding lights, the smell of ether,
      the odor of blood,
    The crowd, O the crowd of the bloody forms, the yard outside
      also fill'd,
    Some on the bare ground, some on planks or stretchers, some in
      the death-spasm sweating,
    An occasional scream or cry, the doctor's shouted orders or calls,
    The glisten of the little steel instruments catching the glint of the
      torches,
20   These I resume as I chant, I see again the forms, I smell the odor,
    Then hear outside the orders given, *Fall in, my men, fall in;*
    But first I bend to the dying lad, his eyes open, a half-smile gives
      he me,
    Then the eyes close, calmly close, and I speed forth to the
      darkness,
    Resuming, marching, ever in darkness marching, on in the ranks,
25   The unknown road still marching.

                                                    1865

Year That Trembled and Reel'd Beneath Me[1]

Year that trembled and reel'd beneath me!
Your summer wind was warm enough, yet the air I breathed froze
    me,
A thick gloom fell through the sunshine and darken'd me,
Must I change my triumphant songs? said I to myself,
5   Must I indeed learn to chant the cold dirges of the baffled?
And sullen hymns of defeat?

                                                    1865

---

[1]The year is probably the crisis year 1863–1864
when the outcome of the Civil War was not at
all certain.

Ethiopia Saluting the Colors[1]

Who are you dusky woman, so ancient hardly human,
With your woolly-white and turban'd head, and bare bony feet?
Why rising by the roadside here, do you the colors greet?

('Tis while our army lines Carolina's sands and pines,
5 Forth from thy hovel door thou Ethiopia com'st to me,
As under doughty Sherman[2] I march toward the sea.)

Me master years a hundred since from my parents sunder'd,
A little child, they caught me as the savage beast is caught,
Then hither me across the sea the cruel slaver brought.

10 No further does she say, but lingering all the day,
Her high-borne turban'd head she wags, and rolls her darkling eye,
And courtesies to the regiments, the guidons moving by.

What is it fateful woman, so blear, hardly human?
Why wag your head with turban bound, yellow, red and green?
15 Are the things so strange and marvelous you see or have seen?

1870

Reconciliation

Word over all, beautiful as the sky,
Beautiful that war and all its deeds or carnage must in time be
    utterly lost,
That the hands of the sisters Death and Night incessantly softly
    wash again, and ever again, this soil'd world;
For my enemy is dead, a man divine as myself is dead,
5 I look where he lies white-faced and still in the coffin—I draw
    near,
Bend down and touch lightly with my lips the white face in the
    coffin.

1865–66

As I Lay with My Head in Your Lap Camerado[1]

As I lay with my head in your lap camerado,
The confession I made I resume, what I said to you and the open
    air I resume,

---

[1]Whitman uses Ethiopia as a generic name for Africa or the black race.
[2]Whitman is referring to General William Sherman's famous march from Atlanta to Sa-vannah in 1864; his army was followed by many black refugees seeking freedom.
[1]Spanish for comrade.

I know I am restless and make others so,
I know my words are weapons full of danger, full of death,
5 For I confront peace, security, and all the settled laws, to unsettle
    them,
I am more resolute because all have denied me than I could ever
    have been had all accepted me,
I heed not and have never heeded either experience, cautions,
    majorities, nor ridicule,
And the threat of what is call'd hell is little or nothing to me,
And the lure of what is call'd heaven is little or nothing to me;
10 Dear camerado! I confess I have urged you onward with me, and
    still urge you, without the least idea what is our destination,
Or whether we shall be victorious, or utterly quell'd and defeated.

1865–66

Memories of President Lincoln[1]

When Lilacs Last in the Dooryard Bloom'd[2]

1

When lilacs last in the dooryard bloom'd,
And the great star early droop'd in the western sky in the night,[3]
I mourn'd, and yet shall mourn with ever-returning spring.

Ever-returning spring, trinity sure to me you bring,
5 Lilac blooming perennial and drooping star in the west,
And thought of him I love.

2

O powerful western fallen star!
O shades of night—O moody, tearful night!
O great star disappear'd—O the black murk that hides the star!

---

[1]This is the only place that Lincoln is specifically named as the subject of these poems.
[2]"Lilacs" was written immediately following
Lincoln's death. He was shot on Good Friday,
April 14, 1865, by John Wilkes Booth; he died
the next morning. In a long procession
through various American cities, his body was
carried by train back to Springfield, Illinois,
where he was buried on May 4, 1865.
[3]The "great star" is the Western star, Venus.

10 O cruel hands that hold me powerless—O helpless soul of me!
    O harsh surrounding cloud that will not free my soul.

3

In the dooryard fronting an old farm-house near the white-wash'd
        palings,
Stands the lilac-bush tall-growing with heart-shaped leaves of rich
        green,
With many a pointed blossom rising delicate, with the perfume
        strong I love,
15 With every leaf a miracle—and from this bush in the dooryard,
    With delicate-color'd blossoms and heart-shaped leaves of rich
        green,
    A sprig with its flower I break.

4

In the swamp in secluded recesses,
A shy and hidden bird is warbling a song.

20 Solitary the thrush,
    The hermit withdrawn to himself, avoiding the settlements,
    Sings by himself a song.

Song of the bleeding throat,
Death's outlet song of life, (for well dear brother I know,
25 If thou wast not granted to sing thou would'st surely die.)

5

Over the breast of the spring, the land, amid cities,
Amid lanes and through old woods, where lately the violets peep'd
        from the ground, spotting the gray debris,
Amid the grass in the fields each side of the lanes, passing the
        endless grass,
Passing the yellow-spear'd wheat, every grain from its shroud in
        the dark-brown fields uprisen,
30 Passing the apple-tree blows of white and pink in the orchards,
    Carrying a corpse to where it shall rest in the grave,
    Night and day journeys a coffin.

6

Coffin that passes through lanes and streets,
Through day and night with the great cloud darkening the land,
35 With the pomp of the inloop'd flags with the cities draped in
        black,
    With the show of the States themselves as of crape-veil'd women
        standing,

With processions long and winding and the flambeaus[4] of the
 night,
With the countless torches lit, with the silent sea of faces and the
 unbared heads,
With the waiting depot, the arriving coffin, and the sombre faces,
40 With dirges through the night, with the thousand voices rising
 strong and solemn,
With all the mournful voices of the dirges pour'd around the
 coffin,
The dim-lit churches and the shuddering organs—where amid
 these you journey,
With the tolling tolling bells' perpetual clang,
Here, coffin that slowly passes,
45 I give you my sprig of lilac.

7

(Nor for you, for one alone,
Blossoms and branches green to coffins all I bring,
For fresh as the morning, thus would I chant a song for you O
 sane and sacred death.

All over bouquets of roses,
50 O death, I cover you over with roses and early lilies,
But mostly and now the lilac that blooms the first,
Copious I break, I break the sprigs from the bushes,
With loaded arms I come, pouring for you,
For you and the coffins all of you O death.)

8

55 O western orb sailing the heaven,
Now I know what you must have meant as a month since I
 walk'd,
As I walk'd in silence the transparent shadowy night,
As I saw you had something to tell as you bent to me night after
 night,
As you droop'd from the sky low down as if to my side, (while the
 other stars all look'd on,)
60 As we wander'd together the solemn night, (for something I know
 not what kept me from sleep,)
As the night advanced, and I saw on the rim of the west how full
 you were of woe,
As I stood on the rising ground in the breeze in the cool
 transparent night,
As I watch'd where you pass'd and was lost in the netherward
 black of the night,

[4]Large candlesticks.

As my soul in its trouble dissatisfied sank, as where you sad orb,
65 Concluded, dropt in the night, and was gone.

9

Sing on there in the swamp,
O singer bashful and tender, I hear your notes, I hear your call,
I hear, I come presently, I understand you,
But a moment I linger, for the lustrous star has detain'd me,
70 The star my departing comrade holds and detains me.

10

O how shall I warble myself for the dead one there I loved?
And how shall I deck my song for the large sweet soul that has
    gone?
And what shall my perfume be for the grave of him I love?

Sea-winds blown from east and west,
75 Blown from the Eastern sea and blown from the Western sea, till
    there on the prairies meeting,
These and with these and the breath of my chant,
I'll perfume the grave of him I love.

11

O what shall I hang on the chamber walls?
And what shall the pictures be that I hang on the walls,
80 To adorn the burial-house of him I love?

Pictures of growing spring and farms and homes,
With the Fourth-month eve at sundown, and the gray smoke lucid
    and bright,
With floods of the yellow gold of the gorgeous, indolent, sinking
    sun, burning, expanding the air,
With the fresh sweet herbage under foot, and the pale green leaves
    of the trees prolific,
85 In the distance the flowing glaze, the breast of the river, with a
    wind-dapple here and there,
With ranging hills on the banks, with many a line against the sky,
    and shadows,
And the city at hand with dwellings so dense, and stacks of
    chimneys,
And all the scenes of life and the workshops, and the workmen
    homeward returning.

12

Lo, body and soul—this land,
90 My own Manhattan with spires, and the sparkling and hurrying
    tides, and the ships,

The varied and ample land, the South and the North in the light,
    Ohio's shores and flashing Missouri,
And ever the far-spreading prairies cover'd with grass and corn.

Lo, the most excellent sun so calm and haughty,
The violet and purple morn with just-felt breezes,
95 The gentle soft-born measureless light,
The miracle spreading bathing all, the fulfill'd noon,
The coming eve delicious, the welcome night and the stars,
Over my cities shining all, enveloping man and land.

13

Sing on, sing on you gray-brown bird,
100 Sing from the swamps, the recesses, pour your chant from the
        bushes,
Limitless out of the dusk, out of the cedars and pines.

Sing on dearest brother, warble your reedy song,
Loud human song, with voice of uttermost woe.

O liquid and free and tender!
105 O wild and loose to my soul—O wondrous singer!
You only I hear—yet the star holds me, (but will soon depart,)
Yet the lilac with mastering odor holds me.

14

Now while I sat in the day and look'd forth,
In the close of the day with its light and the fields of spring, and
        the farmers preparing their crops,
110 In the large unconscious scenery of my land with its lakes and
        forests,
In the heavenly aerial beauty, (after the perturb'd winds and the
        storms,)
Under the arching heavens of the afternoon swift passing, and the
        voices of children and women,
The many-moving sea-tides, and I saw the ships how they sail'd,
And the summer approaching with richness, and the fields all busy
        with labor,
115 And the infinite separate houses, how they all went on, each with
        its meals and minutia of daily usages,
And the streets how their throbbings throbb'd, and the cities pent—
        lo, then and there,
Falling upon them all and among them all, enveloping me with the
        rest,
Appear'd the cloud, appear'd the long black trail,
And I knew death, its thought, and the sacred knowledge of death.
120 Then with the knowledge of death as walking one side of me,

And the thought of death close-walking the other side of me,
And I in the middle as with companions, and as holding the hands
    of companions,
I fled forth to the hiding receiving night that talks not,
Down to the shores of the water, the path by the swamp in the
    dimness,
125 To the solemn shadowy cedars and ghostly pines so still.

And the singer so shy to the rest receiv'd me,
The gray-brown bird I know receiv'd us comrades three,
And he sang the carol of death, and a verse for him I love.

From deep secluded recesses,
130 From the fragrant cedars and the ghostly pines so still,
Came the carol of the bird.

And the charm of the carol rapt me,
As I held as if by their hands my comrades in the night,
And the voice of my spirit tallied the song of the bird.

135 *Come lovely and soothing death,*
    Undulate round the world, serenely arriving, arriving,
    In the day, in the night, to all, to each,
    Sooner or later delicate death.

    Prais'd be the fathomless universe,
140 *For life and joy, and for objects and knowledge curious,*
    And for love, sweet love—but praise! praise! praise!
    For the sure-enwinding arms of cool-enfolding death.

    Dark mother always gliding near with soft feet,
    Have none chanted for thee a chant of fullest welcome?
145 *Then I chant it for thee, I glorify thee above all,*
    I bring thee a song that when thou must indeed come, come
    unfalteringly.

    Approach strong deliveress,
    When it is so, when thou hast taken them I joyously sing the dead,
    Lost in the loving floating ocean of thee,
150 *Laved in the flood of thy bliss O death.*

    From me to thee glad serenades,
    Dances for thee I propose saluting thee, adornments and feastings for
    thee,
    And the sights of the open landscape and the high-spread sky are
    fitting,
    And life and the fields, and the huge and thoughtful night.

155 *The night in silence under many a star,*
   The ocean shore and the husky whispering wave whose voice I
      know,
   And the soul turning to thee O vast and well-veil'd death,
   And the body gratefully nestling close to thee.

   Over the tree-tops I float thee a song,
160 *Over the rising and sinking waves, over the myriad fields and the*
      prairies wide,
   Over the dense-pack'd cities all and the teeming wharves and ways,
   I float this carol with joy, with joy to thee O death.

15

   To the tally of my soul,
   Loud and strong kept up the gray-brown bird,
165 With pure deliberate notes spreading filling the night.

   Loud in the pines and cedars dim,
   Clear in the freshness moist and the swamp-perfume,
   And I with my comrades there in the night.

   While my sight that was bound in my eyes unclosed,
170 As to long panoramas of visions.

   And I saw askant the armies,
   I saw as in noiseless dreams hundreds of battle-flags,
   Borne through the smoke of the battles and pierc'd with missiles I
      saw them,
   And carried hither and yon through the smoke, and torn and
      bloody,
175 And at last but a few shreds left on the staffs, (and all in silence,)
   And the staffs all splinter'd and broken.

   I saw battle-corpses, myriads of them,
   And the white skeletons of young men, I saw them,
   I saw the debris and debris of all the slain soldiers of the war,
180 But I saw they were not as was thought,
   They themselves were fully at rest, they suffer'd not,
   The living remain'd and suffer'd, the mother suffer'd,
   And the wife and the child and the musing comrade suffer'd,
   And the armies that remain'd suffer'd.

16

185 Passing the visions, passing the night,
   Passing, unloosing the hold of my comrades' hands,

Passing the song of the hermit bird and the tallying song of my
    soul,
Victorious song, death's outlet song, yet varying ever-altering song,
As low and wailing, yet clear the notes, rising and falling, flooding
    the night,
190 Sadly sinking and fainting, as warning and warning, and yet again
    bursting with joy,
Covering the earth and filling the spread of the heaven,
As that powerful psalm in the night I heard from recesses,
Passing, I leave thee lilac with heart-shaped leaves,
I leave thee there in the door-yard, blooming, returning with
    spring.

195 I cease from my song for thee,
From my gaze on thee in the west, fronting the west, communing
    with thee,
O comrade lustrous with silver face in the night.
Yet each to keep and all, retrievements out of the night,
The song, the wondrous chant of the gray-brown bird,
200 And the tallying chant, the echo arous'd in my soul,
With the lustrous and drooping star with the countenance full of
    woe,
With the holders holding my hand nearing the call of the bird,
Comrades mine and I in the midst, and their memory ever to
    keep, for the dead I loved so well,
For the sweetest, wisest soul of all my days and lands—and this
    for his dear sake,
205 Lilac and star and bird twined with the chant of my soul,
There in the fragrant pines and the cedars dusk and dim.

1865–66

Autumn Rivulets

Sparkles from the Wheel

Where the city's ceaseless crowd moves on the livelong day,
Withdrawn I join a group of children watching, I pause aside with
    them.

By the curb toward the edge of the flagging,
A knife-grinder works at his wheel sharpening a great knife,

5 Bending over he carefully holds it to the stone, by foot and knee,
With measur'd tread he turns rapidly, as he presses with light but
    firm hand,
Forth issue then in copious golden jets,
Sparkles from the wheel.

The scene and all its belongings, how they seize and affect me,
10 The sad sharp-chinn'd old man with worn clothes and broad
    shoulder-band of leather,
Myself effusing and fluid, a phantom curiously floating, now here
    absorb'd and arrested,
The group, (an unminded point set in a vast surrounding,)
The attentive, quiet children, the loud, proud, restive base of the
    streets,
The low hoarse purr of the whirling stone, the light-press'd blade,
15 Diffusing, dropping, sideways-darting, in tiny showers of gold,
Sparkles from the wheel.

                                        1871

Prayer of Columbus[1]

A batter'd, wreck'd old man,
Thrown on this savage shore, far, far from home,
Pent by the sea and dark rebellious brows, twelve dreary months,
Sore, stiff with many toils, sicken'd and nigh to death,
5 I take my way along the island's edge,
Venting a heavy heart.

I am too full of woe!
Haply I may not live another day;
I cannot rest O God, I cannot eat or drink or sleep,
10 Till I put forth myself, my prayer, once more to Thee,
Breathe, bathe myself once more in Thee, commune with Thee,
Report myself once more to Thee.

Thou knowest my years entire, my life,
My long and crowded life of active work, not adoration merely;
15 Thou knowest the prayers and vigils of my youth,
Thou knowest my manhood's solemn and visionary meditations,
Thou knowest how before I commenced I devoted all to come to
    Thee,
Thou knowest I have in age ratified all those vows and strictly
    kept them,

---

[1]Whitman describes the hardships of Columbus on the island of Jamaica, where he was
ship-wrecked in his attempt to sail around the
world.

Thou knowest I have not once lost nor faith nor ecstasy in Thee,
20 In shackles, prison'd, in disgrace, repining not,
Accepting all from Thee, as duly come from Thee.

All my emprises[2] have been fill'd with Thee,
My speculations, plans, begun and carried on in thoughts of Thee,
Sailing the deep or journeying the land for Thee;
25 Intentions, purports, aspirations mine, leaving results to Thee.

O I am sure they really came from Thee,
The urge, the ardor, the unconquerable will,
The potent, felt, interior command, stronger than words,
A message from the Heavens whispering to me even in sleep,
30 These sped me on.

By me and these the work so far accomplish'd,
By me earth's elder cloy'd and stifled lands uncloy'd, unloos'd,
By me the hemispheres rounded and tied, the unknown to the
        known.

The end I know not, it is all in Thee,
35 Or small or great I know not—haply what broad fields, what
        lands,
Haply the brutish measureless human undergrowth I know,
Transplanted there may rise to stature, knowledge worthy Thee,
Haply the swords I know may there indeed be turn'd to reaping-
        tools,
Haply the lifeless cross I know, Europe's dead cross, may bud and
        blossom there.

40 One effort more, my altar this bleak sand;
That Thou O God my life hast lighted,
With ray of light, steady, ineffable, vouchsafed of Thee,
Light rare untellable, lighting the very light,
Beyond all signs, descriptions, languages;
45 For that O God, be it my latest word, here on my knees,
Old, poor, and paralyzed, I thank Thee.

My terminus near,
The clouds already closing in upon me,
The voyage balk'd, the course disputed, lost,
50 I yield my ships to Thee.
My hands, my limbs grow nerveless,

2Daring adventures.

My brain feels rack'd, bewilder'd,
Let the old timbers part, I will not part,
I will cling fast to Thee, O God, though the waves buffet me,
55 Thee, Thee at least I know.

Is it the prophet's thought I speak, or am I raving?
What do I know of life? what of myself?
I know not even my own work past or present,
Dim ever-shifting guesses of it spread before me,
60 Of newer better worlds, their mighty parturition,
Mocking, perplexing me.

And these things I see suddenly, what mean they?
As if some miracle, some hand divine unseal'd my eyes,
Shadowy vast shapes smile through the air and sky,
65 And on the distant waves sail countless ships,
And anthems in new tongues I hear saluting me.

1874

Whispers of Heavenly Death

Quicksand Years[1]

Quicksand years that whirl me I know not whither,
Your schemes, politics, fail, lines give way, substances mock and
    elude me,
Only the theme I sing, the great and strong-possess'd soul, eludes
    not,
One's-self must never give way—that is the final substance—that
    out of all is sure,
5 Out of politics, triumphs, battles, life, what at last finally remains?
When shows break up what but One's-Self is sure?

1865

---

[1]The poem was drafted in 1862–1863.

From Noon to Starry Night

To a Locomotive in Winter

Thee for my recitative,
Thee in the driving storm even as now, the snow, the winter-day
    declining,
Thee in thy panoply, thy measur'd dual throbbing and thy beat
    convulsive,
Thy black cylindric body, golden brass and silvery steel,
5 Thy ponderous side-bars, parallel and connecting rods, gyrating,
    shuttling at thy sides,
Thy metrical, now swelling pant and roar, now tapering in the
    distance,
Thy great protruding head-light fix'd in front,
Thy long, pale, floating vapor-pennants, tinged with delicate
    purple,
The dense and murky clouds out-belching from thy smoke-stack,
10 Thy knitted frame, thy springs and valves, the tremulous twinkle of
    thy wheels,
Thy train of cars behind, obedient, merrily following,
Through gale or calm, now swift, now slack, yet steadily careering;
Type of the modern—emblem of motion and power—pulse of the
    continent,
For once come serve the Muse and merge in verse, even as here I
    see thee,
15 With storm and buffeting gusts of wind and falling snow,
By day thy warning ringing bell to sound its notes,
By night thy silent signal lamps to swing.

Fierce-throated beauty!
Roll through my chant with all thy lawless music, thy swinging
    lamps at night,
20 Thy madly-whistled laughter, echoing, rumbling like an earth-
    quake, rousing all,
Law of thyself complete, thine own track firmly holding,
(No sweetness debonair of tearful harp or glib piano thine,)
Thy trills of shrieks by rocks and hills return'd,
Launch'd o'er the prairies wide, across the lakes,
25 To the free skies unpent and glad and strong.

1876

Songs of Parting

So Long![1]

To conclude, I announce what comes after me.

I remember I said before my leaves sprang at all,
I would raise my voice jocund and strong with reference to
consummations.

When America does what was promis'd,
5   When through these States walk a hundred millions of superb
persons,
When the rest part away for superb persons and contribute to
them,
When breeds of the most perfect mothers denote America,
Then to me and mine our due fruition.

I have press'd through in my own right,
10   I have sung the body and the soul, war and peace have I sung,
and the songs of life and death,
And the songs of birth, and shown that there are many births.

I have offer'd my style to every one, I have journey'd with
confident step;
While my pleasure is yet at the full I whisper *So long!*
And take the young woman's hand and the young man's hand for
the last time.

15   I announce natural persons to arise,
I announce justice triumphant,
I announce uncompromising liberty and equality,
I announce the justification of candor and the justification of
pride.
I announce that the identity of these States is a single identity only,
20   I announce the Union more and more compact, indissoluble,
I announce splendors and majesties to make all the previous
politics of the earth insignificant.

I announce adhesiveness,[2] I say it shall be limitless, unloosen'd,

[1] In the mid-nineteenth century, "So Long" was an idiomatic expression much used among sailors and street people. This poem concluded *Leaves of Grass* in 1860 and in all subsequent editions.

[2] A term Whitman borrowed from phrenology meaning, he said, the "passion of friendship for man."

I say you shall yet find the friend you were looking for.

I announce a man or woman coming, perhaps you are the one, (*So
long!*)
25 I announce the great individual, fluid as Nature, chaste,
affectionate, compassionate, fully arm'd.

I announce a life that shall be copious, vehement, spiritual, bold,
I announce an end that shall lightly and joyfully meet its
translation.

I announce myriads of youths, beautiful, gigantic, sweet-blooded,
I announce a race of splendid and savage old men.

30 O thicker and faster—(*So long!*)
O crowding too close upon me,
I foresee too much, it means more than I thought,
It appears to me I am dying.

Hasten throat and sound your last,
35 Salute me—salute the days once more. Peal the old cry once more.

Screaming electric, the atmosphere using,
At random glancing, each as I notice absorbing,
Swiftly on, but a little while alighting,
Curious envelop'd messages delivering,
40 Sparkles hot, seed ethereal down in the dirt dropping,
Myself unknowing, my commission obeying, to question it never
daring,
To ages and ages yet the growth of the seed leaving,
To troops out of the war arising, they the tasks I have set
promulging,
To women certain whispers of myself bequeathing, their affection
me more clearly explaining,
45 To young men my problems offering—no dallier I—I the muscle
of their brains trying,
So I pass, a little time vocal, visible, contrary,
Afterward a melodious echo, passionately bent for, (death making
me really undying,)
The best of me then when no longer visible, for toward that I have
been incessantly preparing.

What is there more, that I lag and pause and crouch extended
with unshut mouth?
50 Is there a single final farewell?

My songs cease, I abandon them,
From behind the screen where I hid I advance personally solely to you.

Camerado, this is no book,
Who touches this touches a man,
55 (Is it night? are we here together alone?)
It is I you hold and who holds you,
I spring from the pages into your arms—decease calls me forth.

O how your fingers drowse me,
Your breath falls around me like dew, your pulse lulls the tympans
    of my ears,
60 I feel immerged from head to foot,
Delicious, enough.

Enough O deed impromptu and secret,
Enough O gliding present—enough O summ'd-up past.

Dear friend whoever you are take this kiss,
65 I give it especially to you, do not forget me,
I feel like one who has done work for the day to retire awhile,
I receive now again of my many translations, from my avataras
    ascending, while others doubtless await me,
An unknown sphere more real than I dream'd, more direct, darts
    awakening rays about me, *So long!*
Remember my words, I may again return,
70 I love you, I depart from materials,
I am as one disembodied, triumphant, dead.

                                                    1860

Sands at Seventy (First Annex)

Yonnondio

[The sense of the word is lament for the aborigines. *It is an Iroquois term; and has been used for a personal name.]*

A song, a poem of itself—the word itself a dirge,
Amid the wilds, the rocks, the storm and wintry night,
To me such misty, strange tableaux the syllables calling up;
Yonnondio—I see, far in the west or north, a limitless ravine, with
    plains and mountains dark,
5 I see swarms of stalwart chieftains, medicine-men, and warriors,
As flitting by like clouds of ghosts, they pass and are gone in the
    twilight,
(Race of the woods, the landscapes free, and the falls!
No picture, poem, statement, passing them to the future:)
Yonnondio! Yonnondio!—unlimn'd they disappear;

10 To-day gives place, and fades—the cities, farms, factories fade;
    A muffled sonorous sound, a wailing word is borne through the air
        for a moment,
    Then blank and gone and still, and utterly lost.

1887

Good-bye My Fancy (Second Annex)

Good-bye My Fancy!

Good-bye my Fancy!
Farewell dear mate, dear love!
I'm going away, I know not where,
Or to what fortune, or whether I may ever see you again,
5 So Good-bye my Fancy.

Now for my last—let me look back a moment;
The slower fainter ticking of the clock is in me,
Exit, nightfall, and soon the heart-thud stopping.

Long have we lived, joy'd, caress'd together;
10 Delightful!—now separation—Good-bye my Fancy.

Yet let me not be too hasty,
Long indeed have we lived, slept, filter'd, become really blended
        into one;
Then if we die we die together, (yes, we'll remain one,)
If we go anywhere we'll go together to meet what happens,
15 May-be we'll be better off and blither, and learn something,
May-be it is yourself now really ushering me to the true songs,
        (who knows?)
May-be it is you the mortal knob really undoing, turning—so now
        finally,
Good-bye—and hail! my Fancy.

1891

Respondez!¹

Poem Deleted from Leaves of Grass

Respondez! Respondez!
(The war is completed—the price is paid—the title is settled
    beyond recall;)
Let every one answer! let those who sleep be waked! let none
    evade!
Must we still go on with our affectations and sneaking?
5 Let me bring this to a close—I pronounce openly for a new
    distribution of roles;
Let that which stood in front go behind! and let that which was
    behind advance to the front and speak;
Let murderers, bigots, fools, unclean persons, offer new
    propositions!
Let the old propositions be postponed!
Let faces and theories be turn'd inside out! let meanings be freely
    criminal, as well as results!
10 Let there be no suggestion above the suggestion of drudgery!
Let none be pointed toward his destination! (Say! do you know
    your destination?)
Let men and women be mock'd with bodies and mock'd with
    Souls!
Let the love that waits in them, wait! let it die, or pass still-born
    to other spheres!
Let the sympathy that waits in every man, wait! or let it also pass,
    a dwarf, to other spheres!
15 Let contradictions prevail! let one thing contradict another! and let
    one line of my poems contradict another!
Let the people sprawl with yearning, aimless hands! let their
    tongues be broken! let their eyes be discouraged! let none
    descend into their hearts with the fresh lusciousness of love!
(Stifled, O days! O lands! in every public and private corruption!
Smother'd in thievery, impotence, shamelessness, mountain-high;
Brazen effrontery, scheming, rolling like ocean's waves around and
    upon you, O my days! my lands!
20 For not even those thunderstorms, nor fiercest lightnings of the
    war, have purified the atmosphere;)
—Let the theory of America still be management, caste,
    comparison! (Say! what other theory would you?)

¹Initially entitled "Poem of the Propositions of Nakedness," this poem first appeared in the 1856 edition of *Leaves of Grass.* Later entitled "Respondez," it was deleted from *Leaves of Grass* in 1881.

Let them that distrust birth and death still lead the rest! (Say! why shall they not lead you?)

Let the crust of hell be neared and trod on! let the days be darker than the nights! let slumber bring less slumber than waking time brings!

Let the world never appear to him or her for whom it was all made!

25 Let the heart of the young man still exile itself from the heart of the old man! and let the heart of the old man be exiled from that of the young man!

Let the sun and moon go! let scenery take the applause of the audience! let there be apathy under the stars!

Let freedom prove no man's inalienable right! every one who can tyrannize, let him tyrannize to his satisfaction!

Let none but infidels be countenanced!

Let the eminence of meanness, treachery, sarcasm, hate, greed, indecency, impotence, lust, be taken for granted above all! let writers, judges, governments, households, religions, philosophies, take such for granted above all!

30 Let the worst men beget children out of the worst women!

Let the priest still play at immortality!

Let death be inaugurated!

Let nothing remain but the ashes of teachers, artists, moralists, lawyers, and learn'd and polite persons!

Let him who is without my poems be assassinated!

35 Let the cow, the horse, the camel, the garden-bee—let the mud-fish, the lobster, the mussel, eel, the sting-ray, and the grunting pig-fish—let these, and the like of these, be put on a perfect equality with man and woman!

Let churches accommodate serpents, vermin, and the corpses of those who have died of the most filthy of diseases!

Let marriage slip down among fools, and be for none but fools!

Let men among themselves talk and think forever obscenely of women! and let women among themselves talk and think obscenely of men!

Let us all, without missing one, be exposed in public, naked, monthly, at the peril of our lives! let our bodies be freely handled and examined by whoever chooses!

40 Let nothing but copies at second hand be permitted to exist upon the earth!

Let the earth desert God, nor let there ever henceforth be mention'd the name of God!

Let there be no God!

Let there be money, business, imports, exports, custom, authority, precedents, pallor, dyspepsia, smut, ignorance, unbelief!

Let judges and criminals be transposed! let the prison-keepers be put in prison! let those that were prisoners take the keys!

(Say! why might they not just as well be transposed?)

45 Let the slaves be masters! let the masters become slaves!

Let the reformers descend from the stands where they are forever
bawling! let an idiot or insane person appear on each of the
stands!

Let the Asiatic, the African, the European, the American, and the
Australian, go armed against the murderous stealthiness of
each other! let them sleep armed! let none believe in good
will!

Let there be no unfashionable wisdom! let such be scorn'd and
derided off from the earth!

Let a floating cloud in the sky—let a wave of the sea—let growing
mint, spinach, onions, tomatoes—let these be exhibited as
shows, at a great price for admission!

50 Let all the men of These States stand aside for a few smouchers!
let the few seize on what they choose! let the rest gawk,
giggle, starve, obey!

Let shadows be furnish'd with genitals! let substances be deprived
of their genitals!

Let there be wealthy and immense cities—but still through any of
them, not a single poet, savior, knower, lover!

Let the infidels of These States laugh all faith away!

If one man be found who has faith, let the rest set upon him!

55 Let them affright faith! let them destroy the power of breeding
faith!

Let the she-harlots and the he-harlots be prudent! let them dance
on, while seeming lasts! (O seeming! seeming! seeming!)

Let the preachers recite creeds! let them still teach only what they
have been taught!

Let insanity still have charge of sanity!

Let books take the place of trees, animals, rivers, clouds!

60 Let the daub'd portraits of heroes supersede heroes!

Let the manhood of man never take steps after itself!

Let it take steps after eunuchs, and after consumptive and genteel
persons!

Let the white person again tread the black person under his heel!
(Say! which is trodden under heel, after all?)

Let the reflections of the things of the world be studied in
mirrors! let the things themselves still continue unstudied!

65 Let a man seek pleasure everywhere except in himself!

Let a woman seek happiness everywhere except in herself!

(What real happiness have you had one single hour through your
whole life?)

Let the limited years of life do nothing for the limitless years of
death! (What do you suppose death will do, then?)

1856

from Democratic Vistas[1]

As the greatest lessons of Nature through the universe are perhaps the lessons of variety and freedom, the same present the greatest lessons also in New World politics and progress. If a man were ask'd, for instance, the distinctive points contrasting modern European and American political and other life with the old Asiatic cultus, as lingering-bequeath'd yet in China and Turkey, he might find the amount of them in John Stuart Mill's profound essay on Liberty in the future, where he demands two main constituents, or sub-strata, for a truly grand nationality—1st, a large variety of character—and 2d, full play for human nature to expand itself in numberless and even conflicting directions—(seems to be for general humanity much like the influences that make up, in their limitless field, that perennial health-action of the air we call the weather—an infinite number of currents and forces, and contributions, and temperatures, and cross purposes, whose ceaseless play of counterpart upon counterpart brings constant restoration and vitality.) With this thought—and not for itself alone, but all it necessitates, and draws after it—let me begin my speculations.

America, filling the present with greatest deeds and problems, cheerfully accepting the past, including feudalism, (as, indeed, the present is but the legitimate birth of the past, including feudalism,) counts, as I reckon, for her justification and success, (for who, as yet, dare claim success?) almost entirely on the future. Nor is that hope unwarranted. To-day, ahead, though dimly yet, we see, in vistas, a copious, sane, gigantic offspring. For our New World I consider far less important for what it has done, or what it is, than for results to come. Sole among nationalities, these States have assumed the task to put in forms of lasting power and practicality, on areas of amplitude rivaling the operations of the physical kosmos, the moral political speculations of ages, long, long deferr'd, the democratic republican principle, and the theory of development and perfection by voluntary standards, and self-reliance. Who else, indeed, except the United States, in history, so far, have accepted in unwitting faith, and, as we now see, stand, act upon, and go security for, these things?

But preluding no longer, let me strike the key-note of the following strain. First premising that, though the passages of it have been written at widely different times, (it is, in fact, a collection of memoranda, perhaps for future designers, comprehenders,) and though it may be open to the charge of one part contradicting another—for there are opposite sides to the great question of democracy, as to every great question—I feel the parts harmoniously blended in my own realization and convictions, and present them to be read only in such oneness, each page and each claim and assertion modified and temper'd by the others. Bear in mind, too, that they are not the result of studying up in political economy, but of the ordinary sense, observing,

---

[1]*Democratic Vistas* was written in response to Thomas Carlyle's critique of democracy in "Shooting Niagara" (1867). In this essay, Carlyle described democratic enfranchisement as an unchaining of the devil—or a suicidal leap over Niagara Falls. Sections of this essay, originally entitled "Democracy" and "Personalism," appeared in the New York *Galaxy* in 1867–1868. *Democratic Vistas* was published as a pamphlet in 1871.

wandering among men, these States, these stirring years of war and peace. I will not gloss over the appalling dangers of universal suffrage in the United States. In fact, it is to admit and face these dangers I am writing. To him or her within whose thought rages the battle, advancing, retreating, between democracy's convictions, aspirations, and the people's crudeness, vice, caprices, I mainly write this essay. I shall use the words America and democracy as convertible terms. Not an ordinary one is the issue. The United States are destined either to surmount the gorgeous history of feudalism, or else prove the most tremendous failure of time. Not the least doubtful am I on any prospects of their material success. The triumphant future of their business, geographic and productive departments, on larger scales and in more varieties than ever, is certain. In those respects the republic must soon (if she does not already) outstrip all examples hitherto afforded, and dominate the world. . . .

For my part, I would alarm and caution even the political and business reader, and to the utmost extent, against the prevailing delusion that the establishment of free political institutions, and plentiful intellectual smartness, with general good order, physical plenty, industry, &c., (desirable and precious advantages as they all are,) do, of themselves, determine and yield to our experiment of democracy the fruitage of success. With such advantages at present fully, or almost fully, possess'd—the Union just issued, victorious, from the struggle with the only foes it need ever fear, (namely, those within itself, the interior ones,) and with unprecedented materialistic advancement—society, in these States, is canker'd, crude, superstitious, and rotten. Political, or law-made society is, and private, or voluntary society, is also. In any vigor, the element of the moral conscience, the most important, the verteber to State or man, seems to me either entirely lacking, or seriously enfeebled or ungrown.

I say we had best look our times and lands searchingly in the face, like a physician diagnosing some deep disease. Never was there, perhaps, more hollowness at heart than at present, and here in the United States. Genuine belief seems to have left us. The underlying principles of the States are not honestly believ'd in, (for all this hectic glow, and these melo-dramatic screamings,) nor is humanity itself believ'd in. What penetrating eye does not everywhere see through the mask? The spectacle is appalling. We live in an atmosphere of hypocrisy throughout. The men believe not in the women, nor the women in the men. A scornful superciliousness rules in literature. The aim of all the *littérateurs* is to find something to make fun of. A lot of churches, sects, &c., the most dismal phantasms I know, usurp the name of religion. Conversation is a mass of badinage. From deceit in the spirit, the mother of all false deeds, the offspring is already incalculable. An acute and candid person, in the revenue department in Washington, who is led by the course of his employment to regularly visit the cities, north, south and west, to investigate frauds, has talk'd much with me about his discoveries. The depravity of the business classes of our country is not less than has been supposed, but infinitely greater. The official services of America, national, state, and municipal, in all their branches and departments, except the judiciary, are saturated in corruption, bribery, falsehood, mal-administration; and the judiciary is tainted. The great cities reek with respectable as much as non-respectable robbery and scoundrelism. In fashionable life, flippancy, tepid amours, weak infidelism, small aims, or no aims at all, only to kill time. In business, (this all-devouring modern word, business,) the one sole object is, by any means, pecuniary gain. The magician's serpent in the fable ate up all the other serpents; and money-making is our magician's serpent, remaining to-day sole master of the field. The best class we show, is but a mob of fashionably dress'd speculators and vulgarians. True, indeed, behind this fantastic farce, enacted on the visible stage of society, solid things and stupendous labors are to be discover'd, existing crudely and going on in the background, to advance and tell themselves in time. Yet the truths are none the less terrible. I say that our New World democracy, however great a success in uplifting the masses out of their sloughs, in materialistic development, products, and in a certain highly-deceptive superficial popular intellectuality, is, so far, an almost complete failure in its social aspects, and in really grand religious, moral, literary, and esthetic results. In vain do we march with unprecedented strides to empire so colossal, outvying the antique, beyond Alexander's, beyond the proudest sway of Rome. In vain have we annex'd Texas, California, Alaska, and reach north for Canada and south for Cuba. It is as if we were somehow being endow'd with a vast and more and more thoroughly-appointed body, and then left with little or no soul. . . .

Confess that to severe eyes, using the moral microscrope upon humanity, a sort of dry and flat Sahara appears, these cities, crowded with petty grotesques, malformations, phantoms, playing meaningless antics. Confess that everywhere, in shop, street, church, theatre, bar-room, official chair, are pervading flippancy and vulgarity, low cunning, infidelity—everywhere the youth puny, impudent, foppish, prematurely ripe—everywhere an abnormal libidinousness, unhealthy forms, male, female, painted, padded, dyed, chignon'd, muddy complexions, bad blood, the capacity for good motherhood deceasing or deceas'd, shallow notions of beauty, with a range of manners, or rather lack of manners, (considering the advantages enjoy'd,) probably the meanest to be seen in the world.[2]

Of all this, and these lamentable conditions, to breathe into them the breath recuperative of sane and heroic life, I say a new founded literature, not merely to copy and reflect existing surfaces, or pander to what is called taste—not only to amuse, pass away time, celebrate the beautiful, the refined, the past, or exhibit technical, rhythmic, or grammatical dexterity—but a literature underlying life, religious, consistent with science, handling the elements and forces with competent power, teaching and training men—and, as perhaps the most precious of its results, achieving the entire redemption of woman out of these incredible holds and webs of silliness,

---

[2]Of these rapidly-sketch'd hiatuses, the two which seem to me most serious are, for one, the condition, absence, or perhaps the singular abeyance, of moral conscientious fibre all through American society; and, for another, the appalling depletion of women in their powers of sane athletic maternity, their crowning attribute, and ever making the woman, in loftiest spheres, superior to the man.

I have sometimes thought, indeed, that the sole avenue and means of a reconstructed sociology depended, primarily, on a new birth, elevation, expansion, invigoration of woman, affording, for races to come, (as the conditions that antedate birth are indispensable,) a perfect motherhood. Great, great, indeed, far greater than they know, is the sphere of women. But doubtless the question of such new sociology all goes together, includes many varied and complex influences and premises, and the man as well as the woman, and the woman as well as the man. [Whitman's note]

millinery, and every kind of dyspeptic depletion—and thus insuring to the States a strong and sweet Female Race, a race of perfect Mothers—is what is needed.

And now, in the full conception of these facts and points, and all that they infer, pro and con—with yet unshaken faith in the elements of the American masses, the composites, of both sexes, and even consider'd as individuals—and ever recognizing in them the broadest bases of the best literary and esthetic appreciation—I proceed with my speculations, Vistas. . . .

I say the mission of government, henceforth, in civilized lands, is not repression alone, and not authority alone, not even of law, nor by that favorite standard of the eminent writer, the rule of the best men, the born heroes and captains of the race, (as if such ever, or one time out of a hundred, get into the big places, elective or dynastic)—but higher than the highest arbitrary rule, to train communities through all their grades, beginning with individuals and ending there again, to rule themselves. What Christ appear'd for in the moral-spiritual field for human-kind, namely, that in respect to the absolute soul, there is in the possession of such by each single individual, something so transcendent, so incapable of gradations, (like life,) that, to that extent, it places all beings on a common level, utterly regardless of the distinctions of intellect, virtue, station, or any height or lowliness whatever—is tallied in like manner, in this other field, by democracy's rule that men, the nation, as a common aggregate of living identities, affording in each a separate and complete subject for freedom, worldly thrift and happiness, and for a fair chance for growth, and for protection in citizenship, &c., must, to the political extent of the suffrage or vote, if no further, be placed, in each and in the whole, on one broad, primary, universal, common platform. . . .

Democracy too is law, and of the strictest, amplest kind. Many suppose, (and often in its own ranks the error,) that it means a throwing aside of law, and running riot. But, briefly, it is the superior law, not alone that of physical force, the body, which, adding to, it supersedes with that of the spirit. Law is the unshakable order of the universe forever; and the law over all, and law of laws, is the law of successions; that of the superior law, in time, gradually supplanting and overwhelming the inferior one. (While, for myself, I would cheerfully agree—first covenanting that the formative tendencies shall be administer'd in favor, or at least not against it, and that this reservation be closely construed—that until the individual or community show due signs, or be so minor and fractional as not to endanger the State, the condition of authoritative tutelage may continue, and self-government must abide its time.) Nor is the esthetic point, always an important one, without fascination for highest aiming souls. The common ambition strains for elevations, to become some privileged exclusive. The master sees greatness and health in being part of the mass; nothing will do as well as common ground. Would you have in yourself the divine, vast, general law? Then merge yourself in it.

And, topping democracy, this most alluring record, that it alone can bind, and ever seeks to bind, all nations, all men, of however various and distant lands, into a brotherhood, a family. It is the old, yet ever-modern dream of earth, out of her eldest and her youngest, her fond philosophers and poets. Not that half only, individualism, which isolates. There is another half, which is adhesiveness or love, that fuses, ties and aggregates, making the races comrades, and fraternizing all. Both are to be vitalized by religion, (sole worthiest elevator of man or State,) breathing into the proud, material tissues, the breath of life. For I say at the core of democracy, finally, is the religious element. All the religions, old and new, are there. Nor may the scheme step forth, clothed in resplendent beauty and command, till these, bearing the best, the latest fruit, the spiritual, shall fully appear.

A portion of our pages we might indite with reference toward Europe, especially the British part of it, more than our own land, perhaps not absolutely needed for the home reader. But the whole question hangs together, and fastens and links all peoples. The liberalist of to-day has this advantage over antique or medieval times, that his doctrine seeks not only to individualize but to universalize. The great word Solidarity has arisen. Of all dangers to a nation, as things exist in our day, there can be no greater one than having certain portions of the people set off from the rest by a line drawn—they not privileged as others, but degraded, humiliated, made of no account. Much quackery teems, of course, even on democracy's side, yet does not really affect the orbic quality of the matter. To work in, if we may so term it, and justify God, his divine aggregate, the People, (or, the veritable horn'd and sharp-tail'd Devil, *his* aggregate, if there be who convulsively insist upon it)—this, I say, is what democracy is for; and this is what our America means, and is doing—may I not say, has done? If not, she means nothing more, and does nothing more, than any other land. And as, by virtue of its kosmical, antiseptic power, Nature's stomach is fully strong enough not only to digest the morbific matter always presented, not to be turn'd aside, and perhaps, indeed, intuitively gravitating thither—but even to change such contributions into nutriment for highest use and life—so American democracy's. That is the lesson we, these days, send over to European lands by every western breeze.

And, truly, whatever may be said in the way of abstract argument, for or against the theory of a wider democratizing of institutions in any civilized country, much trouble might well be saved to all European lands by recognizing this palpable fact, (for a palpable fact it is,) that some form of such democratizing is about the only resource now left. *That,* or chronic dissatisfaction continued, mutterings which grow annually louder and louder, till, in due course, and pretty swiftly in most cases, the inevitable crisis, crash, dynastic ruin. Anything worthy to be call'd statesmanship in the Old World, I should say, among the advanced students, adepts, or men of any brains, does not debate to-day whether to hold on, attempting to lean back and monarchize, or to look forward and democratize—but *how,* and in what degree and part, most prudently to democratize. . . .

The true gravitation-hold of liberalism in the United States will be a more universal ownership of property, general homesteads, general comfort—a vast, intertwining reticulation of wealth. As the human frame, or, indeed, any object in this manifold universe, is best kept together by the simple miracle of its own cohesion, and the necessity, exercise and profit thereof, so a great and varied nationality, occupying millions of square miles, were firmest held and knit by the principle of the safety and endurance of the aggregate of its middling property owners. So that, from another point of view, ungracious as it may sound, and a paradox after what we have been saying, democracy looks with suspicious, ill-satisfied eye upon the very poor, the ignorant, and on those out of business. She asks for men and women with occupations, well-off, owners of houses and acres, and with cash in the bank—and with some cravings for literature, too; and must have them, and hastens to make them. Luckily, the seed is already well-sown, and has taken ineradicable root.[3] . . .

America has yet morally and artistically originated nothing. She seems singularly unaware that the models of persons, books, manners, &c., appropriate for former conditions and for European lands, are but exiles and exotics here. No current of her life, as shown on the surfaces of what is authoritatively called her society, accepts or runs into social or esthetic democracy; but all the currents set squarely against it. Never, in the Old World, was thoroughly upholster'd exterior appearance and show, mental and other, built entirely on the idea of caste, and on the sufficiency of mere outside acquisition—never were glibness, verbal intellect, more the test, the emulation—more loftily elevated as head and sample—than they are on the surface of our republican States this day. The writers of a time hint the mottoes of its gods. The word of the modern, say these voices, is the word Culture.

We find ourselves abruptly in close quarters with the enemy. This word Culture, or what it has come to represent, involves, by contrast, our whole theme, and has been, indeed, the spur, urging us to engagement. Certain questions arise. As now taught, accepted and carried out, are not the processes of culture rapidly creating a class of supercilious infidels, who believe in nothing? Shall a man lose himself in countless masses of adjustments, and be so shaped with reference to this, that, and the other, that the simply good and healthy and brave parts of him are reduced and clipp'd away, like the bordering of box in a garden? You can cultivate corn and roses and orchards—but who shall cultivate the mountain peaks, the ocean, and the tumbling gorgeousness of the clouds? Lastly—is the readily-given reply that culture only seeks to help, systematize, and put in attitude, the elements of fertility and power, a conclusive reply?

I do not so much object to the name, or word, but I should certainly insist, for the purposes of these States, on a radical change of category, in the distribution of precedence. I should demand a programme of culture, drawn out, not for a single class alone, or for the parlors or lecture-rooms, but with an eye to practical life, the west, the working-men, the facts of farms and jack-planes and engineers, and of the broad range of the women also of the middle and working strata, and with reference to the perfect equality of women, and of a grand and powerful motherhood. I should demand of this programme or theory a scope generous enough to include the widest human area. It must have for its spinal meaning the formation of a typical personality of character, eligible to the uses of the high average of men—and *not* restricted by

---

[3]For fear of mistake, I may as well distinctly specify, as cheerfully included in the model and standard of these Vistas, a practical, stirring, worldly, money-making, even materialistic character. It is undeniable that our farms, stores, offices, dry-goods, coal and groceries, enginery, cash-accounts, trades, earnings, markets, &c., should be attended to in earnest, and actively pursued, just as if they had a real and permanent existence. I perceive clearly that the extreme business energy, and this almost maniacal appetite for wealth prevalent in the United States, are parts of amelioration and progress, indispensably needed to prepare the very results I demand. My theory includes riches, and the getting of riches, and the amplest products, power, activity, inventions, movements, &c. Upon them, as upon substrata, I raise the edifice design'd in these Vistas. [Whitman's note]

conditions ineligible to the masses. The best culture will always be that of the manly and courageous instincts, and loving perceptions, and of self-respect—aiming to form, over this continent, an idiocrasy of universalism, which, true child of America, will bring joy to its mother, returning to her in her own spirit, recruiting myriads of offspring, able, natural, perceptive, tolerant, devout believers in her, America, and with some definite instinct why and for what she has arisen, most vast, most formidable of historic births, and is, now and here, with wonderful step, journeying through Time. . . .

Of course, in these States, for both man and woman, we must entirely recast the types of highest personality from what the oriental, feudal, ecclesiastical worlds bequeath us, and which yet possess the imaginative and esthetic fields of the United States, pictorial and melodramatic, not without use as studies, but making sad work, and forming a strange anachronism upon the scenes and exigencies around us. Of course, the old undying elements remain. The task is, to successfully adjust them to new combinations, our own days. Nor is this so incredible. I can conceive a community, to-day and here, in which, on a sufficient scale, the perfect personalities, without noise meet; say in some pleasant western settlement or town, where a couple of hundred best men and women, of ordinary worldly status, have by luck been drawn together, with nothing extra of genius or wealth, but virtuous, chaste, industrious, cheerful, resolute, friendly and devout. I can conceive such a community organized in running order, powers judiciously delegated—farming, building, trade, courts, mails, schools, elections, all attended to; and then the rest of life, the main thing, freely branching and blossoming in each individual, and bearing golden fruit. I can see there, in every young and old man, after his kind, and in every woman after hers, a true personality, develop'd, exercised proportionately in body, mind, and spirit. I can imagine this case as one not necessarily rare or difficult, but in buoyant accordance with the municipal and general requirements of our times. And I can realize in it the culmination of something better than any stereotyped éclat of history or poems. Perhaps, unsung, undramatized, unput in essays or biographies—perhaps even some such community already exists, in Ohio, Illinois, Missouri, or somewhere, practically fulfilling itself, and thus outvying, in cheapest vulgar life, all that has been hitherto shown in best ideal pictures. . . .

There are still other standards, suggestions, for products of high literatuses. That which really balances and conserves the social and political world is not so much legislation, police, treaties, and dread of punishment, as the latent eternal intuitional sense, in humanity, of fairness, manliness, decorum, &c. Indeed, this perennial regulation, control, and oversight, by self-suppliance, is *sine qua non* to democracy; and a highest widest aim of democratic literature may well be to bring forth, cultivate, brace, and strengthen this sense, in individuals and society. A strong mastership of the general inferior self by the superior self, is to be aided, secured, indirectly, but surely, by the literatus, in his works, shaping, for individual or aggregate democracy, a great passionate body, in and along with which goes a great masterful spirit.

And still, providing for contingencies, I fain confront the fact, the need of powerful native philosophs and orators and bards, these States, as rallying points to come, in times of danger, and to fend off ruin and defection. For history is long, long, long. Shift and turn the combinations of the statement as we may, the problem of the future of America is in certain respects as dark as it is vast. Pride, competition, segregation, vicious wilfulness, and license beyond example, brood already upon us. Unwieldy and immense, who shall hold in behemoth? who bridle leviathan? Flaunt it as we choose, athwart and over the roads of our progress loom huge uncertainty, and dreadful, threatening gloom. It is useless to deny it: Democracy grows rankly up the thickest, noxious, deadliest plants and fruits of all—brings worse and worse invaders—needs newer, larger, stronger, keener compensations and compellers.

Our lands, embracing so much, (embracing indeed the whole, rejecting none,) hold in their breast that flame also, capable of consuming themselves, consuming us all. Short as the span of our national life has been, already have death and downfall crowded close upon us—and will again crowd close, no doubt, even if warded off. Ages to come may never know, but I know, how narrowly during the late secession war—and more than once, and more than twice or thrice—our Nationality, (wherein bound up, as in a ship in a storm, depended, and yet depend, all our best life, all hope, all value,) just grazed, just by a hair escaped destruction. Alas! to think of them! the agony and bloody sweat of certain of those hours! those cruel, sharp, suspended crises!

Even to-day, amid these whirls, incredible flippancy, and blind fury of parties, infidelity, entire lack of first-class captains and leaders, added to the plentiful meanness and vulgarity of the ostensible masses—that problem, the labor question, beginning to open like a yawning gulf, rapidly widening every year—what prospect have we? We sail a dangerous sea of seething currents, cross and under-currents, vortices—all so dark, untried—and whither shall we turn? It seems as if the Almighty had spread before this nation charts of imperial destinies, dazzling as the sun, yet with many a deep intestine difficulty, and human aggregate of cankerous imperfection,—saying, lo! the roads, the only plans of development, long and varied with all terrible balks and ebullitions. You said in your soul, I will be empire of empires, overshadowing all else, past and present, putting the history of old-world dynasties, conquests behind me, as of no account—making a new history, a history of democracy, making old history a dwarf—I alone inaugurating largeness, culminating time. If these, O lands of America, are indeed the prizes, the determinations of your soul, be it so. But behold the cost, and already specimens of the cost. Thought you greatness was to ripen for you like a pear? If you would have greatness, know that you must conquer it through ages, centuries—must pay for it with a proportionate price. For you too, as for all lands, the struggle, the traitor, the wily person in office, scrofulous wealth, the surfeit of prosperity, the demonism of greed, the hell of passion, the decay of faith, the long postponement, the fossil-like lethargy, the ceaseless need of revolutions, prophets, thunderstorms, deaths, births, new projections and invigorations of ideas and men.

Yet I have dream'd, merged in that hidden-tangled problem of our fate, whose long unraveling stretches mysteriously through time—dream'd out, portray'd, hinted already—a little or a larger band—a band of brave and true, unprecedented yet—arm'd and equipt at every point—the members separated, it may be, by different dates and States, or south, or north, or east, or west—Pacific, Atlantic, Southern, Canadian—a year, a century here, and other centuries there—but always one, compact in soul, conscience-conserving, God-inculcating, inspired achievers, not only in literature, the greatest art, but achievers in all art—a new, undying order, dynasty, from age to age transmitted—a band, a class, at least as fit to cope with current years, our dangers, needs, as those who, for their times, so long, so well, in armor or in cowl, upheld and made illustrious, that far-back feudal, priestly world. To offset chivalry, indeed, those vanish'd countless knights, old altars, abbeys, priests, ages and strings of ages, a knightlier and more sacred cause to-day demands, and shall supply, in a New World, to larger, grander work, more than the counterpart and tally of them.

Arrived now, definitely, at an apex for these Vistas, I confess that the promulgation and belief in such a class or institution—a new and greater literatus order—its possibility, (nay certainty,) underlies these entire speculations—and that the rest, the other parts, as superstructures, are all founded upon it. It really seems to me the condition, not only of our future national and democratic development, but of our perpetuation. In the highly artificial and materialistic bases of modern civilization, with the corresponding arrangements and methods of living, the force-infusion of intellect alone, the depraving influences of riches just as much as poverty, the absence of all high ideals in character—with the long series of tendencies, shapings, which few are strong enough to resist, and which now seem, with steam-engine speed, to be everywhere turning out the generations of humanity like uniform iron castings—all of which, as compared with the feudal ages, we can yet do nothing better than accept, make the best of, and even welcome, upon the whole, for their oceanic practical grandeur, and their restless wholesale kneading of the masses—I say of all this tremendous and dominant play of solely materialistic bearings upon current life in the United States, with the results as already seen, accumulating, and reaching far into the future, that they must either be confronted and met by at least an equally subtle and tremendous force-infusion for purposes of spiritualization, for the pure conscience, for genuine esthetics, and for absolute and primal manliness and womanliness—or else our modern civilization, with all its improvements, is in vain, and we are on the road to a destiny, a status, equivalent, in its real world, to that of the fabled damned.

Prospecting thus the coming unsped days, and that new order in them—marking the endless train of exercise, development, unwind, in nation as in man, which life is for—we see, fore-indicated, amid these prospects and hopes, new law-forces of spoken and written language—not merely the pedagogue-forms, correct, regular, familiar with precedents, made for matters of outside propriety, fine words, thoughts definitely told out—but a language fann'd by the breath of Nature, which leaps overhead, cares mostly for impetus and effects, and for what it plants and invigorates to grow—tallies life and character, and seldomer tells a thing than suggests or necessitates it. In fact, a new theory of literary composition for imaginative works of the very first class, and especially for highest poems, is the sole course open to these States. Books are to be call'd for, and supplied, on the assumption that the process of reading is not a halfsleep, but, in highest sense, an exercise, a gymnast's struggle; that the reader is to do something for himself, must be on the alert, must himself or herself construct indeed the poem, argument, history, metaphysical essay—the text furnishing the hints, the clue, the start or frame-work. Not the book needs so much to be the complete thing, but the reader of the book does. That were to make a nation of supple and athletic minds, well-train'd, intuitive, used to depend on themselves, and not on a few coteries of writers.

Investigating here, we see, not that it is a little thing we have, in having the bequeath'd libraries, countless shelves of volumes, records, &c.; yet how serious the danger, depending entirely on them, of the bloodless vein, the nerveless arm, the false application, at second or third hand. We see that the real interest of this people of ours in the theology, history, poetry, politics, and personal models of the past, (the British islands, for instance, and indeed all the past,) is not necessarily to mould ourselves or our literature upon them, but to attain fuller, more definite comparisons, warnings, and the insight to ourselves, our own present, and our own far grander, different, future history, religion, social customs, &c. We see that almost everything that has been written, sung, or stated, of old, with reference to humanity under the feudal and oriental institutes, religions, and for other lands, needs to be re-written, resung, re-stated, in terms consistent with the institution of these States, and to come in range and obedient uniformity with them.

We see, as in the universes of the material kosmos, after meteorological, vegetable, and animal cycles, man at last arises, born through them, to prove them, concentrate them, to turn upon them with wonder and love—to command them, adorn them, and carry them upward into superior realms—so, out of the series of the preceding social and political universes, now arise these States. We see that while many were supposing things established and completed, really the grandest things always remain; and discover that the work of the New World is not ended, but only fairly begun.

We see our land, America, her literature, esthetics, &c., as, substantially, the getting in form, or effusement and statement, of deepest basic elements and loftiest final meanings, of history and man—and the portrayal, (under the eternal laws and conditions of beauty,) of our own physiognomy, the subjective tie and expression of the objective, as from our own combination, continuation, and points of view—and the deposit and record of the national mentality, character, appeals, heroism, wars, and even liberties—where these, and all, culminate in native literary and artistic formulation, to be perpetuated; and not having which native, first-class formulation, she will flounder about, and her other, however imposing, eminent greatness, prove merely a passing gleam; but truly having which, she will understand herself, live nobly, nobly contribute, emanate, and, swinging, poised safely on herself, illumin'd and illuming, become a full-form'd world, and divine Mother not only of material but spiritual worlds, in ceaseless succession through time—the main thing being the average, the bodily, the concrete, the democratic, the popular, on which all the superstructures of the future are to permanently rest.

1871

Emily Dickinson 1830–1886

For Emily Dickinson, the immeasurable, unrecorded life was far more real than the verifiable one; the intersections of visible and invisible worlds far more electric than facts recognized by biographers. A sketch of her known dates and places cannot capture or account for Dickinson's extraordinary sensibility or originality, which brought fresh currents into American thought and literature and expanded the possibilities of poetry.

Dickinson lived in Amherst, Massachusetts, where she was born in 1830 and died in 1886. She shared her family's household with her younger sister Lavinia, her mother, Emily Norcross Dickinson, and her father, Edward Dickinson, a lawyer, congressman, and treasurer of Amherst College. Her brother Austin, one year older, a lawyer like his father, lived for most of his life in the house nextdoor, after marrying Dickinson's friend Susan Huntington Gilbert. We know few details about Dickinson's mother: she had a year of higher education, rather unusual for a woman in the early nineteenth century; like Emily, she was a skilled and avid gardener; she shared domestic responsibilities with her daughters, and Lavinia took on much of the household management.

Squire Edward Dickinson emerges as a dominant and domineering figure in the family, whom Emily Dickinson seems to have both honored and humored. To her brother Austin, away at law school, she wrote:

> We dont have *many jokes tho'* now, *it is pretty much all sobriety, and we do not have much poetry, father having made up his mind that its pretty much all* real *life. Fathers real life and* mine *sometimes come into collision, but as yet, escape unhurt!* . . .

About ten years later she wrote to a friend: "He buys me many Books—but begs me not to read them—because he fears they joggle the Mind." Dickinson implied that her parents neither comprehended nor aided her development, but we know that their quiet style of living, their secure economic class, and perhaps even their emotional remoteness allowed her the privacy in which to develop her writing. Lavinia protected that privacy, and said after Dickinson's death that Emily was the one of the family who had *thinking* to do.

By the age of twelve, Dickinson was a fluent and prolific writer of letters. Austin described the dramatic effect of her talent at Amherst Academy and Mount Holyoke Female Seminary (now Mount Holyoke College), where she spent one year. "Her compositions were unlike anything ever heard—and always produced a sensation—both with the scholars and Teachers—her imagination sparkled—and she gave it free rein. She was full of courage—but always had a peculiar personal sensitiveness. She saw things directly and just as they were. She abhorred sham. . . ."

Dickinson's early letters reveal a witty, startling, irreverent imagination, and a passion for situations which combined friendship, honesty, secrecy, private jokes, and talk about books and ideas. Though her childhood was a time of mass evangelistic conversions, or revivals, in the churches of western Massachusetts, when all souls were urged to commit themselves to Christ, Dickinson refused to think badly of "the world," or believe that greater pleasures could be found in heaven than on earth. Of her family's habits of traditional prayer and churchgoing she wrote, "[They] are religious—except me—and address an Eclipse, every morning—whom they call 'Father.'" Her letters indicate that she found life exhilarating and sufficient, if only it would last, and that for her, heaven was embodied in familiar surroundings, in nature, in love, and in the power of thought.

Why Dickinson spent only one year at Mount Holyoke, we do not know. Her father seems to have wanted her at home. Religious pressure may also have contributed to her departure. Mary Lyon, founder of the Seminary, ranked incoming students on the basis of their spiritual condition, and her staff made separate lists of those who "*had* a hope" (of receiving God's grace), or had "indulged" a hope, or had no hope. Dickinson's name remained on the final list, despite intense public pressure to attend religious meetings and re-examine her soul. Her letters suggest that she refused to profess a sense of sin; such a refusal required an astonishing degree of originality and courage. Her poems and letters indicate that throughout her life she felt she had a direct route to the Infinite, especially through the world of the mind, and that churches, sermons, preachers, revival meetings, and theological vocabulary did not express her sense of eternity, tremendousness, awe, or spiritual center, which she also named Circumference. Attention to her own experience was her great route to the Infinite.

After one year of college, Dickinson made only five or six trips away from Amherst, traveling in her twenty-fifth year with her father to Philadelphia and Washington, and spending time in Boston in her early thirties when she developed an acute eye problem.

For women of Dickinson's class, the appropriate social institutions were the family and the church; with those came many societal obligations. Women of her day were not expected to be intellectuals, leaders, thinkers, philosophers, or creators. But Dickinson rebelled. She was a woman who created her own avenues of thought, providing a striking example of an alternative sensibility, a dissenting imagination, a re-creating mind.

Attenuated doses of society were enough for Dickinson. She found the electricity between two individuals in a room quite overpowering, when it wasn't stifling, and she needed much time for solitude.

Dickinson rarely, if ever, left her family's house and grounds during the last twenty years of her life, but we should not imagine her disconnected from life. The Dickinson family was prominent in the town and the state, and many visitors came to visit at the two Dickinson houses. Susan, Austin, and their children lived next door. The family holdings included gardens, lawns, a meadow, a stream, an oak grove, a barn, and a conservatory. A number of household workers were employed, in-cluding many from among the local community of Irish immigrants. Dickinson's bedroom overlooked the main road from Boston to Amherst, on which there was constant traffic. She could look from the windows of that room, where she wrote most of her poetry, toward the house of her sister-in-law and brother, and toward Amherst College and the town's center with its churches, shops, and citizens coming and going.

We also know that Dickinson was a cosmopolitan and eclectic reader. Her letters indicate that she read newspapers and periodicals, following closely local and national events, and reading contemporary poetry and fiction as soon as it came into print. Many of her letters contain requests to borrow books or offers to loan them. She seems to have learned much of the Bible and Shakespeare by heart; her letters are filled with scriptural and literary allusion. She read women writers with particular passion, including Elizabeth Barrett Browning, George Eliot, the Brontës, Harriet Beecher Stowe, and her own friend, Helen Hunt Jackson, who urged her vehemently, and in vain, to publish her poems.

Dickinson was immensely responsive to friendship with those she found interesting, and loved both women and men with a passionate intensity expressed in both letters and poems. "My friends are my estate," she once wrote. Throughout her life she referred to those she loved as "treasures" and "possessions." For her, friendship was like Heaven, and she resented the Calvinistic God, both "burglar" and "banker," who would jealously take those she loved from her. At the same time, she hoped, and believed with "uncertain certainty," that, after death, God would "refund" her "confiscated Gods."

One whom Dickinson loved was her sister-in-law Susan, a woman with whom she was closely connected from her late teens until her death. As far as we know, Susan received more of Dickinson's writing than any other correspondent. The letters and poems sent across the lawn to Susan are evidence of the intimacy and constancy as well as the tensions of this friendship. Those inclined to view Dickinson as emotionally impoverished might think instead of her living for three decades next door to the woman, also a writer, to whom she wrote: "With the exception of Shakespeare, you have told me of more knowledge than any one living—To say that sincerely is strange praise."

Apparently Austin Dickinson, with his mistress, Mabel Loomis Todd, who was editing the poems for publication, mutilated Dickinson's manuscripts, erasing his wife's name and scissoring out references to her. One poem sent to Susan, "One Sister have I in our house," included in our selection, was completely scratched out, line by line. It seems that Susan, too, withheld information. Only after her death in 1913 did she allow her daughter Martha Dickinson Bianchi to publish poems and letters she had received from Dickinson, and it is possible that this writing to be shared with the world was carefully chosen, while other work was destroyed.

It is important to understand the role in Dickinson studies played by homophobia, which is the fear and hatred of love between people of the same sex. We do not know to what extent Dickinson expressed her sexual desires physically, but we do have clear evidence that her affinities were both lesbian and heterosexual.

One of the most enduring legends in Dickinson studies is the story that the love poems were written to the man Dickinson addressed in several passionate letters as "Master." (It is unclear whether these letters were ever actually sent.) Some argue that "Master" can be identified as the Reverend Charles Wadsworth of Philadelphia and claim that it was Wadsworth who "broke the poet's heart." This story set off the search for "the one true [male] love" of Dickinson's life, which has extended into many contemporary readings of Dickinson.

In the end, though we cannot define the exact nature of Dickinson's bonds with the women and men of her "estate," it is important to realize that she counted each a "treasure." Among them were Benjamin Newton, her early friend; *Springfield Daily Republican* editor Samuel Bowles, his wife Mary, and his cousin Maria Whitney; Judge Otis Lord, a family friend in love with her and she with him late in her life; Mrs. Holland, whom she addressed as "Little Sister"; the writer and reformer Thomas Wentworth Higginson, whom she called her "Mentor." Each to her was a rare object of love and desire, as well as a source of intellectual stimulation and an audience for her writing.

At the age of 31, Dickinson sent several poems to Higginson, responding to his "Letter to a Young Contributor" in *The Atlantic Monthly.* She asked, "Are you too deeply occupied to say if my Verse is alive?" The Higginson selection in this anthology includes a letter to his wife describing his first visit to Dickinson: "I never was with a person who drained my nerve power so much," he wrote. Even though Higginson stood in awe of the poet, he apparently commented that the poetry was "spasmodic" and "uncontrolled," and despite Dickinson's admiration for her "teacher," she seems never to have taken any of his advice. The only documentation we have of Dickinson ever having taken anyone's suggestions concerning her poems is an exchange of letters in which she sent Susan a requested revision.

Although ten poems by Emily Dickinson were published during her lifetime, we have no evidence that she sought, desired, or welcomed their publication, and considerable evidence that she did not. She enclosed many poems in letters, but no member of the family guessed how seriously she took herself as a poet until after she died, when it was realized that over a period of years she had engaged in what is probably the most remarkable instance of private publication in American letters.

Dickinson copied almost 1,200 poems onto folded sheets of white, unlined stationery, marking with a small "x" certain words and phrases she considered revising, then listed possible alternative word choices at the bottom of the page. She stacked several folded sheets on top of one another, punched two holes, and tied each packet together along one edge with cotton string. Each of the "packets," also called "fascicles" (we have no way of knowing what name Dickinson had for them), contains from 16 to 24 pages and an average of 20 poems. Dickinson's use of and intentions for these packets are unknown. They may have constituted a storage and filing system; some critics believe they have thematic coherence.

Photostatic representations of "fascicle" poems as well as electronic images, in online editions, of unbound poems, drafts, and fragments allow us to study Dickinson's manuscripts, observing, for instance, her exact use of punctuation. She used dashes in the place of more traditional marks, such as periods, commas, colons, and semicolons, and some see it as significant that the dashes vary in length and that some slope upward, some downward. One supposition is that Dickinson may have used the dash to direct a reader to stress certain words and phrases. With the dash, Dickinson could avoid what she may have considered the spurious finality of the period. Photostats of the poems also show us Dickinson's line breaks, now a subject of debate among readers, editors, and critics.

When she died, Dickinson left Lavinia and Maggie Maher, a woman who worked in the household, specific instructions to destroy the letters she had received and saved. She made no mention of her poetry. When Lavinia discovered the poems, she was determined to get them into print, and she persuaded Higginson and Mabel Loomis Todd to edit them. Todd and Higginson published volumes of selected poems in 1890 and 1891; in 1896 Todd edited a third volume. The poems were received with great excitement; the 1890 volume went through seven printings in a year, the 1891 volume five printings in two years. Because of complex family feuds which separated the manuscripts, Dickinson's complete poems and all known variant readings were not published until 1955.

In reading Dickinson's poetry, it is best not to look for creeds or statements of belief. Though she reflects her community's Protestant and Calvinistic frames of reference, religious terminology in her poetry does not indicate that she held orthodox religious beliefs. She is by turn satirical, skeptical, awed, reverent, speculative, outraged, tantalized, ironic, or God-like herself. She scorns theological portraits of "God" but aligns herself personally with divinity, sometimes as Jesus and sometimes as co-creator. Dickinson wrote a remarkable number of poems on pain, a taboo subject in her time and place. She refused to accept the Calvinistic teaching that she had earned pain, through original sin, or the Transcendentalist habit of transcending it, through denial or euphemism. Tracking her experience led her to fearful and dire states of insight, often bordering on madness and despair. She felt appalling losses, which in some cases also brought compensations of knowledge or spiritual insight, but she insisted on recording her perception of pain in language which was unflinching: "I like a look of Agony,/Because I know it's true—"

Dickinson experimented radically with poetic style: she was taut, terse, suggestive, oblique. The words she chose live vividly on the page and invite readers to fill the poems with their own sense of connection. Her tone is often both intimate and stark, especially in the many first lines beginning with "I": "I felt a funeral in my brain . . . ," "I dwell in possibility . . . ," "I measure every grief I meet. . . ." She rearranged word order, ignored rules of punctuation, evaded rhyme schemes even while suggesting them, and in general tried to ventilate and open up language to the point where it approximated her own sense of the layered complexity of matter, spirit, and consciousness. The English sentence as she inherited it must have seemed to her like a blunt instrument. Her meter suggests not certainty or regularity, but mobility, unfinished business, life in motion. Because she rarely rhymed exactly, one critic has suggested that for her, life did not rhyme. But it seems to have come tantalizingly, agonizingly close before it refused.

Certainly Dickinson's explorations of consciousness, and the strategies she used to free language from traditional structures and expectations continue to challenge, reward, and astonish readers year after year. Dickinson was a poet who had the courage to resist many authorities, even at the price of being misunderstood. Wresting language back to the service of her own experience, she gives us glimpses of a person too startling to be acceptable to her community, with a mind too exacting to use language as she had learned it, a heart of unacceptable desires and unanswerable demands, and a sensibility embodying in life and language an early and genuine example of the sometimes illusory American trait of self-reliance.

Peggy McIntosh
Wellesley College, Center for Research on Women

Ellen Louise Hart
University of California at Santa Cruz, Cowell College

PRIMARY WORKS

The Poems of Emily Dickinson, ed. Thomas H. Johnson, 3 vols., 1951, 1955; *The Letters of Emily Dickinson,* ed. Thomas H. Johnson and Theodora Ward, 3 vols., 1958; R. W. Franklin, ed., *The Manuscript Books of Emily Dickinson,* 2 vols., 1981; R. W. Franklin, ed., *The Poems of Emily Dickinson (Variorum Edition),* 3 vols., 1998; R. W. Franklin, ed., *The Poems of Emily Dickinson (Reading Edition),* 1999; Ellen Louise Hart and Martha Nell Smith, eds., *Open Me Carefully: Emily Dickinson's Intimate Letters to Susan Huntington Dickinson,* 1998; Marta Werner, *Radical Scatters: Emily Dickinson's Late Fragments and Related Texts, 1870–1886,* 1999; Dickinson Editing Collective, Martha Nell Smith, coordinator, Ellen Louise Hart and Marta Werner, general editors, Dickinson Electronic Archives, http://jefferson.village. virginia.edu/dickinson.

Poems

One Sister have I in our house,
And one, a hedge away.
There's only one recorded,
But both belong to me.

5 One came the road that I came—
And wore my last year's gown—
The other, as a bird her nest,
Builded our hearts among.

She did not sing as we did—
10 It was a different tune—

Herself to her a music
As Bumble bee of June.

Today is far from Childhood—
But up and down the hills
15 I held her hand the tighter—
Which shortened all the miles—

And still her hum
The years among,
Deceives the Butterfly;
20 Still in her Eye
The Violets lie
Mouldered this many May.

I spilt the dew—
But took the morn—
25 I chose this single star
From out the wide night's numbers—
Sue—forevermore![1]

J. 14   F. 5   1858   1914[2]

I never lost as much but twice,
And that was in the sod.[1]
Twice have I stood a beggar
Before the door of God!

5 Angels—twice descending
Reimbursed my store—
Burglar! Banker—Father!
I am poor once more!

J. 49   F. 39   c. 1858   1890

Success is counted sweetest
By those who ne'er succeed.
To comprehend a nectar[1]
Requires sorest need.

---

[1]This poem was in Fascicle 2, which originally contained 24 poems. Sometime in 1891, it was cancelled out, probably by Austin Dickinson and Mabel Loomis Todd. We have the complete text in a copy sent by Dickinson to Sue Gilbert in 1858.

[2]"J" refers to the number of the poem in the Johnson edition, "F" to the number of the poem in the Franklin edition. The year on the left is the date the poem was written, according to Johnson. If "c." precedes the year, the date is approximate. The year on the right is the earliest date of publication.

[1]The sod: *i.e.*, burial.

[1]Drink of Greek and Roman gods.

5 Not one of all the purple Host
Who took the Flag[2] today
Can tell the definition
So clear of Victory
As he defeated—dying—
10 On whose forbidden ear
The distant strains of triumph
Burst agonized and clear!

J. 67   F. 112   c. 1859   1878

Her breast is fit for pearls,
But I was not a "Diver"—
Her brow is fit for thrones
But I have not a crest.
5 Her heart is fit for *home*—
I—a Sparrow—build there
Sweet of twigs and twine
My perennial nest.

J. 84   F. 121   c. 1859   1894

These are the days when Birds come back—
A very few—a Bird or two—
To take a backward look.
These are the days when skies resume
5 The old—old sophistries[1] of June—
A blue and gold mistake.

Oh fraud that cannot cheat the Bee—
Almost thy plausibility
Induces my belief.

10 Till ranks of seeds their witness bear—
And softly thro' the altered air
Hurries a timid leaf.

Oh Sacrament of summer days,
Oh Last Communion in the Haze—
15 Permit a child to join,

Thy sacred emblems to partake—
Thy consecrated bread to take
And thine immortal wine![2]

J. 130   F. 122   c. 1859   1890

---

[2]Vanquished the enemy.
[1]Deceptive arguments.
[2]Dickinson compares the end of summer to the
last supper of Christ, celebrated in some
churches as the Sacrament of Communion.

Come slowly—Eden!
Lips unused to Thee—
Bashful—sip thy Jessamines—[1]
As the fainting Bee—

5 Reaching late his flower,
Round her chamber hums—
Counts his nectars—
Enters—and is lost in Balms.[2]

J. 211   F. 205   c. 1860   1890

Did the Harebell loose her girdle[1]
To the lover Bee
Would the Bee the Harebell *hallow*
Much as formerly?

5 Did the "Paradise"—persuaded—
Yield her moat of pearl—
Would the Eden *be* an Eden,
Or the Earl—an *Earl?*

J. 213   F. 134   c. 1860   1891

I like a look of Agony,
Because I know it's true—
Men do not sham Convulsion,
Nor simulate, a Throe—

5 The Eyes glaze once—and that is Death—
Impossible to feign
The Beads upon the Forehead
By homely Anguish strung.

J. 241   F. 339   c. 1861   1890

Wild Nights—Wild Nights!
Were I with thee
Wild Nights should be
Our luxury!

5 Futile—the Winds—
To a Heart in port—
Done with the Compass—
Done with the Chart!

---

[1]Jasmines; fragrant flowers.
[2]Healing ointments.
[1]Loosen her sash.

Rowing in Eden—
10 Ah, the Sea!
Might I but moor—Tonight—
In Thee![1]

J. 249   F. 269   c. 1861   1891

I can wade Grief—
Whole Pools of it—
I'm used to that—
But the least push of Joy
5 Breaks up my feet—
And I tip—drunken—
Let no Pebble—smile—
'Twas the New Liquor—
That was all!

10 Power is only Pain—
Stranded, thro' Discipline,
Till Weights—will hang—
Give Balm—to Giants—
And they'll wilt, like Men—
15 Give Himmaleh—[1]
They'll Carry—Him!

J. 252   F. 312   c. 1861   1891

There's a certain Slant of light,
Winter Afternoons—
That oppresses, like the Heft[1]
Of Cathedral Tunes—

5 Heavenly Hurt, it gives us—
We can find no scar,
But internal difference,
Where the Meanings, are—

None may teach it—Any—
10 'Tis the Seal Despair—
An imperial affliction
Sent us of the Air—

When it comes, the Landscape listens—
Shadows—hold their breath—

---

[1]Dickinson juxtaposes stormy nights with lovers' sheltered ports and moorings.

[1]A personification of the Himalayan mountains.
[1]Weight or bulk.

15 When it goes, 'tis like the Distance
  On the look of Death—

    J. 258   F. 320   c. 1861   1890

I felt a Funeral, in my Brain,
And Mourners to and fro
Kept treading—treading—till it seemed
That Sense was breaking through—[1]

5 And when they all were seated,
  A Service, like a Drum—
  Kept beating—beating—till I thought
  My Mind was going numb—

And then I heard them lift a Box
10 And creak across my Soul
  With those same Boots of Lead, again,
  Then Space—began to toll,

As[2] all the Heavens were a Bell,
And Being, but an Ear,
15 And I, and Silence, some strange Race
  Wrecked, solitary, here—

And then a Plank in Reason, broke,
And I dropped down, and down—
And hit a World, at every plunge,
20 And Finished knowing—then—

    J. 280   F. 340   c. 1861   1896

I'm Nobody! Who are you?
Are you—Nobody—too?
Then there's a pair of us!
Dont tell! they'd banish us—you know!

5 How dreary—to be—Somebody!
  How public—like a Frog—
  To tell your name—the livelong June—
  To an admiring Bog!

    J. 288   F. 260   c. 1861   1891

If your Nerve, deny you—
Go above your Nerve—

---

[1] *I.e.,* sense was giving way.
[2] As if. Dickinson often uses "as" in this way.

He can lean against the Grave,
If he fear to swerve—

5 That's a steady posture—
Never any bend
Held of those Brass arms—
Best Giant made—

If your Soul seesaw—
10 Lift the Flesh door—
The Poltroon[1] wants Oxygen—
Nothing more—

J. 292   F. 329   c. 1861   1935

Your Riches—taught me—Poverty.
Myself—a Millionaire
In little Wealths, as Girls could boast
Till broad as Buenos Ayre—[1]

5 You drifted your Dominions—
A Different Peru—
And I esteemed All Poverty
For Life's Estate with you—

Of Mines, I little know—myself—
10 But just the names, of Gems—
The Colors of the Commonest—
And scarce of Diadems—

So much, that did I meet the Queen—
Her Glory I should know—
15 But this, must be a different Wealth—
To miss it—beggars so—

I'm sure 'tis India—all Day—
To those who look on You—
Without a stint—without a blame,
20 Might I—but be the Jew—

I'm sure it is Golconda—[2]
Beyond my power to deem—
To have a smile for Mine—each Day,
How better, than a Gem!

---

[1]Coward.
[1]Buenos Aires, Argentina.
[2]Dickinson associates Latin countries and the ruined city of Golconda in India with gems, gold, and pearls.

25 At least, it solaces to know
  That there exists—a Gold—
  Altho' I prove it, just in time
  It's distance—to behold—

  It's far—far Treasure to surmise—
30 And estimate the Pearl—
  That slipped my simple fingers through—
  While just a Girl at School.

    J. 299   F. 418   1862   1891

  I reason, Earth is short—
  And Anguish—absolute—
  And many hurt,
  But, what of that?

5 I reason, we could die—
  The best Vitality
  Cannot excel Decay,
  But, what of that?

  I reason, that in Heaven—
10 Somehow, it will be even—
  Some new Equation, given—
  But, what of that?

    J. 301   F. 403   c. 1862   1890

  The Soul selects her own Society—
  Then—shuts the Door—
  To her divine Majority—
  Present no more—

5 Unmoved—she notes the Chariots—pausing—
  At her low Gate—
  Unmoved—an Emperor be kneeling
  Upon her Mat—

  I've known her—from an ample nation—
10 Choose One—
  Then—close the Valves of her attention—
  Like Stone—

    J. 303   F. 409   c. 1862   1890

  The Soul's Superior instants
  Occur to Her—alone—
  When friend—and Earth's occasion
  Have infinite withdrawn—

5   Or She—Herself—ascended
    To too remote a Hight
    For lower Recognition
    Than Her Omnipotent—

    This Mortal Abolition[1]
10 Is seldom—but as fair
    As Apparition[2]—subject
    To Autocratic Air—

    Eternity's disclosure
    To favorites—a few—
15 Of the Colossal substance
    Of Immortality

        J. 306   F. 630   c. 1862   1914

    I send Two Sunsets—
    Day and I—in competition ran—
    I finished Two—and several Stars—
    While He—was making One—

5   His own was ampler—but as I
    Was saying to a friend—
    Mine—is the more convenient
    To Carry in the Hand—

        J. 308   F. 557   c. 1862   1914

    It sifts from Leaden Sieves—
    It powders all the Wood.
    It fills with Alabaster Wool
    The Wrinkles of the Road—

5   It makes an Even Face
    Of Mountain, and of Plain—
    Unbroken Forehead from the East
    Unto the East again—

    It reaches to the Fence—
10 It wraps it Rail by Rail
    Till it is lost in Fleeces—
    It deals Celestial Vail

---

[1]Dismissal or rejection of the time-bound.
[2]Vision of an unearthly being.

To Stump, and Stack—and Stem—
A Summer's empty Room—
15 Acres of Joints, where Harvests were,
Recordless, but for them—

It Ruffles Wrists of Posts
As Ankles of a Queen—
Then stills it's Artisans—like Ghosts—
20 Denying they have been—

J. 311   F. 291   c. 1862   1891

There came a Day at Summer's full,
Entirely for me—
I thought that such were for the Saints,
Where Resurrections—be—

5 The Sun, as common, went abroad,
The flowers, accustomed, blew,
As if no soul the solstice passed
That maketh all things new—

The time was scarce profaned, by speech—
10 The symbol of a word
Was needless, as at Sacrament,
The Wardrobe—of our Lord—

Each was to each The Sealed Church,
Permitted to commune this—time—
15 Lest we too awkward show
At Supper of the Lamb.[1]

The Hours slid fast—as Hours will,
Clutched tight, by greedy hands—
So faces on two Decks, look back,
20 Bound to opposing lands—

And so when all the time had leaked,
Without external sound
Each bound the Other's Crucifix—
We gave no other Bond—

25 Sufficient troth, that we shall rise—
Deposed—at length, the Grave—
To that new Marriage,

[1]The Last Supper or Lord's Supper.

Justified—through Calvaries[2] of Love—

J. 322   F. 325   c. 1861   1890

Some keep the Sabbath going to Church—
I keep it, staying at Home—
With a Bobolink for a Chorister—
And an Orchard, for a Dome—

5 Some keep the Sabbath in Surplice[1]—
I just wear my Wings—
And instead of tolling the Bell, for Church,
Our little Sexton[2]—sings.

God preaches, a noted Clergyman—
10 And the sermon is never long,
So instead of getting to Heaven, at last—
I'm going, all along.

J. 324   F. 236   c. 1860   1864

A Bird came down the Walk—
He did not know I saw—
He bit an Angleworm in halves
And ate the fellow, raw,

5 And then he drank a Dew
From a convenient Grass—
And then hopped sidewise to the Wall
To let a Beetle pass—

He glanced with rapid eyes
10 That hurried all around—
They looked like frightened Beads, I thought—
He stirred his Velvet Head

Like one in danger, Cautious,
I offered him a Crumb
15 And he unrolled his feathers
And rowed him softer home—

Than Oars divide the Ocean,
Too silver for a seam—
Or Butterflies, off Banks of Noon

[2]Calvary was the hill outside Jerusalem on   [2]Church custodian and keeper of property.
which Jesus was crucified.
[1]A white gown-like vestment with open sleeves
worn by clergymen at services.

20 Leap, plashless[1] as they swim.

  J. 328 F. 359 c. 1862 1891

  I know that He exists.
  Somewhere—in Silence—
  He has hid his rare life
  From our gross eyes.

5 'Tis an instant's play.
  'Tis a fond Ambush—
  Just to make Bliss
  Earn her own surprise!

  But—should the play
10 Prove piercing earnest—
  Should the glee—glaze—
  In Death's—stiff—stare—

  Would not the fun
  Look too expensive!
15 Would not the jest—
  Have crawled too far!

  J. 338 F. 365 c. 1862 1891

  After great pain, a formal feeling comes—
  The Nerves sit ceremonious, like Tombs—
  The stiff Heart questions was it He, that bore,
  And Yesterday, or Centuries before?

5 The Feet, mechanical, go round—
  Of Ground, or Air, or Ought—[1]
  A Wooden way
  Regardless grown,[2]
  A Quartz contentment, like a stone—

10 This is the Hour of Lead—
  Remembered, if outlived,
  As Freezing persons, recollect the Snow—
  First—Chill—then Stupor—then the letting go—

  J. 341 F. 372 c. 1862 1929

  God is a distant—stately Lover—
  Woos, as He states us—by His Son—

---

[1]Splashless.
[1]Dickinson's spelling of Aught; anything.

[2]Having stopped noticing.

Verily, a Vicarious Courtship—
"Miles", and "Priscilla", were such an One—

5 But, lest the Soul—like fair "Priscilla"
Choose the Envoy—and spurn the Groom—
Vouches, with hyperbolic archness—
"Miles", and "John Alden" were Synonyme—[1]

J. 357   F. 615   c. 1862   1891

Dare you see a Soul *at the White Heat?*
Then crouch within the door—
Red—is the Fire's common tint—
But when the vivid Ore
5 Has vanquished Flame's conditions,
It quivers from the Forge
Without a color, but the light
Of unannointed Blaze.
Least[1] Village has it's Blacksmith
10 Whose Anvil's even ring
Stands symbol for the finer Forge
That soundless tugs—within—
Refining these impatient Ores
With Hammer, and with Blaze
15 Until the Designated Light
Repudiate[2] the Forge—

J. 365   F. 401   c. 1862   1891

What Soft—Cherubic Creatures—
These Gentlewomen are—
One would as soon assault a Plush—[1]
Or violate[2] a Star—

5 Such Dimity[3] Convictions—
A Horror so refined
Of freckled Human Nature—
Of Deity—ashamed—

It's such a common—Glory—
10 A Fisherman's—Degree—[4]
Redemption—Brittle Lady—

---

[1]"Miles": the New England puritan Miles Standish is said to have sent a younger man, John Alden, to propose to Priscilla Mullen for him. Priscilla answered, "Speak for yourself, John," and married the younger man.
[1]The smallest.
[2]Leave behind, disown.

[1]Piece of upholstery material or upholstered furniture.
[2]Rape; desecrate.
[3]Delicate cotton fabric.
[4]*I.e.,* merely having the status of Christ, who was associated with fishing and later symbolized by a fish.

Be so—ashamed of Thee—

J. 401   F. 675   c. 1862   1896

Much Madness is divinest Sense—
To a discerning Eye—
Much Sense—the starkest Madness—
'Tis the Majority
5   In this, as All, prevail—
Assent—and you are sane—
Demur[1]—you're straightway dangerous—
And handled with a Chain—

J. 435   F. 620   c. 1862   1890

This is my letter to the World
That never wrote to Me—
The simple News that Nature told—
With tender Majesty

5   Her Message is committed
To Hands I cannot see—
For love of Her—Sweet—countrymen—
Judge tenderly—of Me[1]

J. 441   F. 519   c. 1862   1890

I tie my Hat—I crease my Shawl—
Life's little duties do—precisely—
As[1] the very least
Were infinite—to me—

5   I put new Blossoms in the Glass—
And throw the old—away—
I push a petal from my Gown
That anchored there—I weigh
The time 'twill be till six o'clock
10 I have so much to do—
And yet—Existence—some way back—
Stopped—struck—my ticking—through—
We cannot put Ourself away
As a completed Man
15 Or Woman—When the Errand's done
We came to Flesh—upon—

---

[1]Disagree.

[1]This poem was placed by Higginson and Todd just after the table of contents and before the first page of selections in the first edition of Dickinson's poetry, published in 1890.

There is no indication that she intended it as an introduction to all of the fascicles; it is lodged in fascicle 24 where it shares a page with part of another poem.

[1]As if.

There may be—Miles on Miles of Nought—
Of Action—sicker far—
To simulate—is stinging work—
20 To cover what we are
From Science—and from Surgery—
Too Telescopic Eyes
To bear on us unshaded—
For their—sake—not for Our's—
25 'Twould start them—
We—could tremble—
But since we got a Bomb—
And held it in our Bosom—
Nay—Hold it—it is calm—

———————[2]

30 Therefore—we do life's labor—
Though life's Reward—be done—
With scrupulous exactness—
To hold our Senses—on—

J. 443   F. 522   c. 1862   1929

I showed her Hights she never saw—
"Would'st Climb," I said?
She said—"Not so"—
"With *me*—" I said—With *me*?
5 I showed her Secrets—Morning's Nest—
The Rope the Nights were put across—
And *now*—"Would'st have me for a Guest?"
She could not find her Yes—
And then, I brake my life—And Lo,
10 A Light, for her, did solemn glow,
The larger, as her face withdrew—
And *could* she, further, "No"?[1]

J. 446   F. 346   c. 1862   1896

This was a Poet—It is That
Distills amazing sense
From Ordinary Meanings—
And Attar[1] so immense

[2]It was unusual for Dickinson to draw a line, as she did here, between parts of a poem.
[1]This copy of the poem was sent to Sue in 1862. In the same year, Dickinson copied the poem into a fascicle, with different pronouns:
  He showed me Hights I never saw

"Would'st Climb," He said?
I said, "Not so."
  "With me—" He said—"With me?" . . .
For further notes, see the Johnson variorum edition.
[1]Perfume obtained by crushing flower petals.

5 From the familiar species
That perished by the Door—
We wonder it was not Ourselves
Arrested it—before—

Of Pictures, the Discloser—
10 The Poet—it is He—
Entitles Us—by Contrast—
To ceaseless Poverty—

Of Portion—so unconscious—
The Robbing—could not harm—[2]
15 Himself—to Him—a Fortune—
Exterior—to Time—

    J. 448   F. 446   c. 1862   1929

I heard a Fly buzz—when I died—
The Stillness in the Room
Was like the Stillness in the Air—
Between the Heaves of Storm—

5 The Eyes around—had wrung them dry—
And Breaths were gathering firm
For that last Onset—when the King
Be witnessed—in the Room—

I willed my Keepsakes—Signed away
10 What portion of me be
Assignable—and then it was
There interposed a Fly—

With Blue—uncertain—stumbling Buzz—
Between the light—and me—
15 And then the Windows failed—and then
I could not see to see—

    J. 465   F. 591   c. 1862   1896

This World is not Conclusion.
A Species stands beyond—
Invisible, as Music—
But positive, as Sound—
5 It beckons, and it baffles—
Philosophy—dont know—

---

[2]So unaware of his treasure that stealing could
not hurt him.

And through a Riddle, at the last—
Sagacity,[1] must go—
To guess it, puzzles scholars—
10 To gain it, Men have borne
Contempt of Generations
And Crucifixion, shown—
Faith slips—and laughs, and rallies—
Blushes, if any see—
15 Plucks at a twig of Evidence—
And asks a Vane,[2] the way—
Much Gesture, from the Pulpit—
Strong Hallelujahs roll—
Narcotics cannot still the Tooth
20 That nibbles at the soul—

J. 501   F. 373   c. 1862   1896

Her sweet Weight on my Heart a Night
Had scarcely deigned to lie—
When, stirring, for Belief's delight,
My Bride had slipped away—

5 If 'twas a Dream—made solid—just
The Heaven to confirm—
Or if Myself were dreamed of Her—
The power to presume—

With Him remain—who unto Me—
10 Gave—even as to All—
A Fiction superseding Faith—
By so much—as 'twas real—

J. 518   F. 611   c. 1862   1945

I started Early—Took my Dog—
And visited the Sea—
The Mermaids in the Basement
Came out to look at me—

5 And Frigates—in the Upper Floor
Extended Hempen Hands—[1]
Presuming Me to be a Mouse—
Aground—upon the Sands—

---

[1]Keenness of sense perception.
[2]Weathervane.
[1]Ropes.

But no Man moved Me—till the Tide
10 Went past my simple Shoe—
And past my Apron—and my Belt
And past my Boddice²—too—

And made as He would eat me up—
As wholly as a Dew
15 Upon a Dandelion's Sleeve—
And then—I started—too—

And He—He followed—close behind—
I felt His Silver Heel
Upon my Ancle—Then my Shoes
20 Would overflow with Pearl—

Until We met the Solid Town—
No One He seemed to know—
And bowing—with a Mighty look—
At me—The Sea withdrew—

J. 520   F. 656   c. 1862   1891

One Crucifixion is recorded—only—
How many be
Is not affirmed of Mathematics—
Or History—

5 One Calvary¹—exhibited to Stranger—
As many be
As Persons—or Peninsulas—
Gethsemane—²

Is but a Province—in the Being's Centre—
10 Judea—³
For Journey—or Crusade's Achieving—
Too near—

Our Lord—indeed—made Compound Witness—⁴
And yet—

²An article of women's clothing laced and worn like a vest over a blouse.
¹Hill of Jesus' crucifixion.
²Garden in which Jesus was arrested before his death.
³The Holy Land.
⁴Had many witnesses.

15 There's newer—nearer Crucifixion
Than That—

J. 553   F. 670   c. 1862   1945

I reckon—when I count at all—
First—Poets—Then the Sun—
Then Summer—Then the Heaven of God—
And then—the List is done—

5 But, looking back—the First so seems
To Comprehend the Whole—
The Others look a needless Show—
So I write—Poets—All—

Their Summer—lasts a Solid Year—
10 They can afford a Sun
The East—would deem extravagant—
And if the Further Heaven—

Be Beautiful as they prepare
For Those who worship Them—
15 It is too difficult a Grace—
To justify the Dream—

J. 569   F. 533   c. 1862   1929

I had been hungry, all the Years—
My Noon had Come—to dine—
I trembling drew the Table near—
And touched the Curious Wine—

5 'Twas this on Tables I had seen—
When turning, hungry, Home
I looked in Windows, for the Wealth
I could not hope—for Mine—

I did not know the ample Bread—
10 'Twas so unlike the Crumb
The Birds and I, had often shared
In Nature's—Dining Room—

The Plenty hurt me—'twas so new—
Myself felt ill—and odd—
15 As Berry—of a Mountain Bush—
Transplanted—to the Road—

Nor was I hungry—so I found
That Hunger—was a way

Of Persons outside Windows—
20 The Entering—takes away—

    J. 579   F. 439   c. 1862   1891

Empty my Heart, of Thee—
It's single Artery—
Begin, and leave Thee out—
Simply Extinction's Date—

5 Much Billow hath the Sea—
One Baltic—They—[1]
Subtract Thyself, in play,
And not enough of me
Is left—to put away—
10 "Myself" meant Thee—

Erase the Root—no Tree—
Thee—then—no me—
The Heavens stripped—
Eternity's vast pocket, picked—

    J. 587   F. 393   c. 1862   1929

They shut me up in Prose—
As when a little Girl
They put me in the Closet—
Because they liked me "still"—

5 Still! Could themself have peeped—
And seen my Brain—go round—
They might as wise have lodged a Bird
For Treason—in the Pound—[1]

Himself has but to will
10 And easy as a Star
Look down upon Captivity—
And laugh—No more have I—[2]

    J. 613   F. 445   c. 1862   1935

Ourselves were wed one summer—dear—
Your Vision—was in June—
And when Your little Lifetime failed,
I wearied—too—of mine—

---

[1] The waves (billows) make one [Baltic] sea.
[1] An enclosure without a roof for livestock or other animals.

[2] *I.e.,* I need do no more than the bird to escape my captivity.

5 And overtaken in the Dark—
Where You had put me down—
By Some one carrying a Light—
I—too—received the Sign.

'Tis true—Our Futures different lay—
10 Your Cottage—faced the sun—
While Oceans—and the North must be—
On every side of mine

'Tis true, Your Garden led the Bloom,
For mine—in Frosts—was sown—
15 And yet, one Summer, we were Queens—
But You—were crowned in June—

      J. 631   F. 596   c. 1862   1945

The Brain—is wider than the Sky—
For—put them side by side—
The one the other will contain
With ease—and You—beside—

5 The Brain is deeper than the sea—
For—hold them—Blue to Blue—
The one the other will absorb—
As Sponges—Buckets—do—

The Brain is just the weight of God—
10 For—Heft them—Pound for Pound—
And they will differ—if they do—
As Syllable from Sound—

      J. 632   F. 598   c. 1862   1896

I cannot live with You—
It would be Life—
And Life is over there—
Behind the Shelf

5 The Sexton[1] keeps the Key to—
Putting up
Our Life—His Porcelain—
Like a Cup—

---

[1]Custodian of church property; bellringer;
grave-digger.

Discarded of the Housewife—
10 Quaint—or Broke—
A newer Sevres[2] pleases—
Old Ones crack—

I could not die—with You—
For One must wait
15 To shut the Other's Gaze down—
You—could not—

And I—Could I stand by
And see You—freeze—
Without my Right of Frost—
20 Death's privilege?

Nor could I rise—with You—
Because Your Face
Would put out Jesus'—
That New Grace

25 Glow plain—and foreign
On my homesick Eye—
Except that You than He
Shone closer by—

They'd judge Us—How—
30 For You—served Heaven—You know,
Or sought to—
I could not—

Because You saturated Sight—
And I had no more Eyes
35 For sordid excellence
As Paradise

And were You lost, I would be—
Though My Name
Rang loudest
40 On the Heavenly fame—

And were You—saved—
And I—condemned to be

---

[2]Fine French porcelain china.

Where You were not—
That self—were Hell to Me—

45 So We must meet apart—
You there—I—here—
With just the Door ajar
That Oceans are—and Prayer—
And that White Sustenance—
50 Despair—

J. 640   F. 706   c. 1862   1890

I dwell in Possibility—
A fairer House than Prose—
More numerous of Windows—
Superior—for Doors—

5 Of Chambers as the Cedars—
Impregnable of Eye—[1]
And for an Everlasting Roof
The Gambrels[2] of the Sky—

Of Visiters—the fairest—
10 For Occupation—This—
The spreading wide my narrow Hands
To gather Paradise—

J. 657   F. 466   c. 1862   1929

Of all the Souls that stand create—
I have elected—One—
When Sense from Spirit—files away—
And Subterfuge—is done—
5 When that which is—and that which was—
Apart—intrinsic—stand—
And this brief Tragedy of Flesh—
Is shifted—like a Sand—
When Figures show their royal Front—
10 And Mists—are carved away,
Behold the Atom—I preferred—

---

[1]Impenetrable, impossible to see through, like some dense cedar trees.   [2]Ridged roofs with two slopes on each side, the lower slope having the steeper pitch.

To all the lists[1] of Clay!

J. 664   F. 279   c. 1862   1891

One need not be a Chamber—to be Haunted—
One need not be a House—
The Brain has Corridors—surpassing
Material Place—
5 Far safer, of a Midnight Meeting
External Ghost
Than it's interior Confronting—
That Cooler Host.

Far safer, through an Abbey gallop,
10 The Stones a' chase—
Than Unarmed, one's a'self encounter—
In lonesome Place—

Ourself behind ourself, concealed—
Should startle most—
15 Assassin hid in our Apartment
Be Horror's least.[1]

The Body—borrows a Revolver—
He bolts the Door—
O'erlooking a superior spectre—[2]
20 Or More—

J. 670   F. 407   c. 1863   1891

Essential Oils—are wrung—
The Attar[1] from the Rose
Be not expressed[2] by Suns—alone—
It is the gift of Screws—

5 The General Rose—decay—
But this—in Lady's Drawer
Make Summer—When the Lady lie
In Ceaseless Rosemary—[3]

J. 675   F. 772   c. 1863   1891

---

[1]Probably in the archaic sense of limits, boundaries, borders.
[1]*I.e.,* should be the least horrifying of the things we fear.
[2]Not seeing that there is a greater ghost within.

[1]Perfume derived from crushing flower petals.
[2]Pressed out, or brought out.
[3]Herb associated with remembrance, or memory.

They say that "Time assuages"—[1]
Time never did assuage—
An actual suffering strengthens
As Sinews do, with age—

5   Time is a Test of Trouble—
But not a Remedy—
If such it prove, it prove too
There was no Malady—

J. 686   F. 861   c. 1863   1896

Publication—is the Auction
Of the Mind of Man—
Poverty—be justifying
For so foul a thing

5   Possibly[1]—but We—would rather
From Our Garret go
White—Unto the White Creator—
Than invest—Our Snow—

Thought belong to Him who gave it—
10 Then—to Him Who bear
It's Corporeal illustration—Sell
The Royal Air—

In the Parcel—Be the Merchant
Of the Heavenly Grace—
15 But reduce no Human Spirit
To Disgrace of Price—

J. 709   F. 788   c. 1863   1929

Because I could not stop for Death—
He kindly stopped for me—
The Carriage held but just Ourselves—
And Immortality.

5   We slowly drove—He knew no haste
And I had put away
My labor and my leisure too,
For His Civility—

[1]Eases or reduces a hurt.
[1]*I.e.,* possibly the alternative of poverty would
justify publication.

We passed the School, where Children strove
10 At Recess—in the Ring—
We passed the Fields of Gazing Grain—
We passed the Setting Sun—

Or rather—He passed Us—
The Dews drew quivering and chill—
15 For only Gossamer,[1] my Gown—
My Tippet[2]—only Tulle—[3]

We paused before a House that seemed
A Swelling of the Ground—
The Roof was scarcely visible—
20 The Cornice[4]—in the Ground—

Since then—'tis Centuries—and yet
Feels shorter than the Day
I first surmised the Horses Heads
Were toward Eternity—

J. 712   F. 479   c. 1863   1890

She rose to His Requirement—dropt
The Playthings of Her Life
To take the honorable Work
Of Woman, and of Wife—

5 If ought[1] She missed in Her new Day,
Of Amplitude, or Awe—
Or first Prospective—Or the Gold
In using, wear away,

It lay unmentioned—as the Sea
10 Develope Pearl, and Weed,
But only to Himself—be known
The Fathoms[2] they abide—

J. 732   F. 857   c. 1863   1890

My Life had stood—a Loaded Gun—
In Corners—till a Day
The Owner passed—identified—
And carried Me away—

---

[1]Very fine fabric.
[2]Shoulder cape.
[3]Thin silk netting.
[4]Molding, often decorative, below the roof of a building.

[1]Aught; anything.
[2]*I.e.,* how deep they lie and in what surroundings. The fathom measures water depth.

5 And now We roam in Sovreign Woods—
   And now We hunt the Doe—
   And every time I speak for Him—
   The Mountains straight reply—

   And do I smile, such cordial light
10 Upon the Valley glow—
   It is as a Vesuvian[1] face
   Had let it's pleasure through—

   And when at Night—Our good Day done—
   I guard My Master's Head—
15 'Tis better than the Eider-Duck's[2]
   Deep Pillow—to have shared—

   To foe of His—I'm deadly foe—
   None stir the second time—
   On whom I lay a Yellow Eye—
20 Or an Emphatic Thumb—

   Though I than He—may longer live
   He longer must—than I—
   For I have but the power to kill,
   Without—the power to die—

   J. 754   F. 764   c. 1863   1929

   Presentiment—is that long Shadow—on the Lawn—
   Indicative that Suns go down—

   The Notice to the startled Grass
   That Darkness—is about to pass—

   J. 764   F. 487   c. 1863   1890

   This Consciousness that is aware
   Of Neighbors and the Sun
   Will be the one aware of Death
   And that itself alone

5 Is traversing the interval
   Experience between
   And most profound experiment
   Appointed unto Men—

---

[1]Volcanic, like Mt. Vesuvius in Italy; capable of
breathing fire, light, and destruction.
[2]*I.e.,* downy (with duck down).

How adequate unto itself
10 It's properties shall be
Itself unto itself and none
Shall make discovery.

Adventure most unto itself
The Soul condemned to be—
15 Attended by a single Hound
It's own identity.
J. 822   F. 819   c. 1864   1945

The Poets light but Lamps—
Themselves—go out—
The Wicks they stimulate—
If vital Light

5 Inhere as do the Suns—
Each Age a Lens
Disseminating their
Circumference—
J. 883   F. 930   c. 1864   1945

The Missing All, prevented Me
From missing minor Things.
If nothing larger than a World's
Departure from a Hinge

5 Or Sun's extinction, be observed
'Twas not so large that I
Could lift my Forehead from my work
For Curiosity.
J. 985   F. 995   c. 1865   1914

A narrow Fellow in the Grass
Occasionally rides—
You may have met Him—did you not
His notice sudden is—

5 The Grass divides as with a Comb—
A spotted Shaft is seen—
And then it closes at your feet
And opens further on—

He likes a Boggy Acre
10 A Floor too cool for Corn—
Yet when a Boy, and Barefoot—
I more than once at Noon

Have passed, I thought, a Whip lash
Unbraiding in the Sun
15   When stooping to secure it
It wrinkled, and was gone—

Several of Nature's People
I know, and they know me—
I feel for them a transport
20   Of Cordiality—

But never met this Fellow
Attended, or alone
Without a tighter breathing
And Zero at the Bone—

J. 986   F. 1096   c. 1865   1866

Perception of an object costs
Precise the Object's loss—
Perception in itself a Gain
Replying to it's Price—

5   The Object Absolute—is nought—
Perception sets it fair
And then upbraids[1] a Perfectness
That situates so far—

J. 1071   F. 1103   c. 1866   1914

Title divine—is mine!
The Wife—without the Sign!
Acute Degree—conferred on me—
Empress of Calvary!
5   Royal—all but the Crown!
Betrothed—without the swoon
God sends us Women—
When you—hold—Garnet to Garnet—
Gold—to Gold—
10   Born—Bridalled—Shrouded—
In a Day—
"My Husband"—women say—
Stroking the Melody—
Is *this*—the way?

J. 1072   F. 194   c. 1862   1924

[1]Reproaches.

The Bustle in a House
The Morning after Death
Is solemnest of industries
Enacted upon Earth—

5 The Sweeping up the Heart
And putting Love away
We shall not want to use again
Until Eternity.

J. 1078   F. 1108   c. 1866   1890

Revolution is the Pod
Systems rattle from
When the Winds of Will are stirred
Excellent is Bloom

5 But except[1] it's Russet[2] Base
Every Summer be
The Entomber of itself,
So of Liberty—

Left inactive on the Stalk
10 All it's Purple fled
Revolution shakes it for
Test if it be dead.

J. 1082   F. 1044   c. 1866   1929

Tell all the Truth but tell it slant—
Success in Circuit lies
Too bright for our infirm Delight
The Truth's superb surprise
5 As Lightning to the Children eased
With explanation kind
The Truth must dazzle gradually
Or every man be blind—

J. 1129   F. 1263   c. 1868   1945

He preached upon "Breadth" till it argued him narrow—
The Broad are too broad to define
And of "Truth" until it proclaimed him a Liar—
The Truth never flaunted a Sign—

---

[1]But for, *i.e.,* if it were not for.
[2]Reddish brown associated with leaves, pods, stalks in autumn.

5 Simplicity fled from his counterfeit presence
As Gold the Pyrites[1] would shun—
What confusion would cover the innocent Jesus
To meet so enabled a Man!

J. 1207   F. 1266   c. 1872   1891

[A worksheet draft of this poem printed below reveals some of Dickinson's
characteristic ways of working. For other examples of variant readings, see the
three-volume Johnson edition and the manuscript books edited by Franklin.]

He preached about Breadth till ~~we~~ knew ~~he was~~ narrow
      upon   *it argued him*
The Broad are too broad to define
And of Truth until it proclaimed him a Liar
The Truth never ~~hoisted~~ a sign—
       flaunted
Simplicity fled from his counterfeit presence
As Gold the Pyrites would shun
    a
What confusion would cover the innocent Jesus
To meet so ~~learned~~ a man—
at meeting   *Religious*
      enabled
    so accomplished
     discerning
     accoutred
     established
     conclusive

Not with a Club, the Heart is broken
Nor with a Stone—
A Whip so small you could not see it
I've known

5 To lash the Magic Creature
Till it fell,
Yet that Whip's Name
Too noble then to tell.

Magnanimous as Bird
10 By Boy descried—[1]
Singing unto the Stone[2]
Of which it died—

[1]A bright, brassy metal known as Fool's Gold.   [2]*I.e.,* stone fired from a slingshot.
[1]Sought out, found.

Shame need not crouch
In such an Earth as Our's—
15 Shame—stand erect—
The Universe is your's.

    J. 1304   F. 1349   c. 1874   1896

What mystery pervades a well!
The water lives so far—
A neighbor from another world
Residing in a jar

5 Whose limit none have ever seen,
But just his lid of glass—
Like looking every time you please
In an abyss's face!

The grass does not appear afraid,
10 I often wonder he
Can stand so close and look so bold
At what is awe to me.

Related somehow they may be,
The sedge stands next the sea—
15 Where he is floorless
And does no timidity betray

But nature is a stranger yet;
The ones that cite her most[1]
Have never passed her haunted house,
20 Nor simplified her ghost.[2]

To pity those that know her not
Is helped by the regret
That those who know her, know her less
The nearer her they get.[3]

    J. 1400   F. 1433   c. 1877   1896

---

[1]Refer to her most often as an authority, example, or proof.
[2]Spirit.
[3]Dickinson sent Sue a variant of the last two stanzas. It is signed "Emily—"and was written about 1877.

    But Susan is a Stranger yet—

The Ones who cite her most
Have never scaled her Haunted House
Nor compromised her Ghost—
To pity those who know her not
Is helped by the regret
That those who know her know her less
The nearer her they get—

A Counterfeit—a Plated Person—
I would not be—
Whatever strata of Iniquity
My Nature underlie—
5   Truth is good Health—and Safety, and the Sky.
How meagre, what an Exile—is a Lie,
And Vocal—when we die—

J. 1453   F. 1514   c. 1879   1924

"Heavenly Father"—take to thee
The supreme iniquity[1]
Fashioned by thy candid Hand
In a moment contraband—[2]
5   Though to trust us—seem to us
More respectful—"We are Dust"—
We apologize to thee
For thine own Duplicity—[3]

J. 1461   F. 1500   c. 1879   1914

A Route of Evanescence
With a revolving Wheel—
A Resonance of Emerald—
A Rush of Cochineal—[1]
5   And every Blossom on the Bush
Adjusts it's tumbled Head—
The mail from Tunis,[2] probably,
An easy Morning's Ride—[3]

J. 1463   F. 1489   c. 1879   1891

The Bible is an antique Volume—
Written by faded Men
At the suggestion of Holy Spectres—
Subjects—Bethlehem—
5   Eden—the ancient Homestead—
Satan—the Brigadier—

[1]Wickedness; sinfulness.
[2]Forbidden moment.
[3]*I.e.,* your doubleness, in creating something and then holding it accountable for the wicked nature you gave it. The quotation marks around "Heavenly Father" and "We are Dust" call attention to the ironic tone of this apology.

[1]Brilliant red dye.
[2]An African city in Tunisia, near the ancient site of Carthage.
[3]Dickinson sent copies of this poem in several letters to friends and referred to it as "A Humming Bird."

Judas—the Great Defaulter—
David—the Troubadour—
Sin—a distinguished Precipice
10 Others must resist—
Boys that "believe" are very lonesome—
Other Boys are "lost"—
Had but the Tale a warbling Teller—
All the Boys would come—
15 Orpheus' Sermon captivated—
It did not condemn—[1]

J. 1545   F. 1577   c. 1882   1924

Volcanoes be in Sicily
And South America
I judge from my Geography
Volcanoes nearer here
5 A Lava step at any time
Am I inclined to climb
A Crater I may contemplate
Vesuvius[1] at Home

J. 1705   F. 1691   ?   1914

Rearrange a "Wife's" affection!
When they dislocate my Brain!
Amputate my freckled Bosom!
Make me bearded like a man!

5 Blush, my spirit, in thy Fastness—
Blush, my unacknowledged clay—
Seven years of troth have taught thee
More than Wifehood ever may!

Love that never leaped its socket—
10 Trust entrenched in narrow pain—
Constancy thro' fire—awarded—
Anguish—bare of anodyne![1]

Burden—borne so far triumphant—
None suspect me of the crown,

[1]Dickinson sent this poem to her nephew Ned Gilbert when he was 21. She entitled an earlier version of the poem "Diagnosis of the Bible, by a Boy—." In Dickinson's view, the Bible's didactic tone alienates many readers.

[1]Mt. Vesuvius, a powerful and active volcano in Italy.
[1]Pain-killing medicine.

15 For I wear the "Thorns"[2] till *Sunset*—
   Then—my Diadem[3] put on.

   Big my Secret but it's *bandaged*—
   It will never get away
   Till the Day its Weary Keeper
20 Leads it through the Grave to thee.[4]

   J. 1737   F. 267   c. 1861   1945

   To make a prairie it takes a clover and one bee,
   One clover, and a bee,
   And revery.
   The revery alone will do,
5 If bees are few.

   J. 1755   F. 1779   ?   1896

Letters

To Abiah Root

29 January 1850

Very dear Abiah.[1]

The folks have all gone away—they thought that they left me alone, and contrived things to amuse me should they stay long, and *I* be lonely. Lonely indeed—they did'nt look, and they could'nt have seen if they had, who should bear me company. *Three* here instead of *one*—would'nt it scare them? A curious trio, part earthly and part spiritual two of us—the other all heaven, and no earth. *God* is sitting here, looking into my very soul to see if I think right tho'ts. Yet I am not afraid, for I try to be right and good, and he knows every one of my struggles. He looks very gloriously, and everything bright seems dull beside him, and I dont dare to look directly at him for fear I shall die. Then *you* are here—dressed in that quiet black gown and cap—that funny little cap I used to laugh at you about, and you dont appear to be thinking about anything in particular, not in one of your *breaking dish* moods I

---

[2]A reference to the crown of thorns which Christ was forced to wear before the crucifixion.

[3]Crown or headband, often of jewels, worn by royalty.

[4]This poem was originally copied into fascicle 11 by Dickinson around 1861. Seven years earlier would have been 1854, a year after Sue be-

came engaged to Austin. The poem was removed from fascicle 11 by someone after Dickinson's death.

[1]Abiah Root was among Dickinson's early circle of friends. Letters to Abiah are intimate and affectionate. No correspondence remains after 1854, the year Abiah Root married.

take it, you seem aware that I'm writing you, and are amused I should think at any such friendly manifestation when you are already present. *Success* however even in making a fool of one's-self is'nt to be despised, so I shall persist in writing, and you may in laughing at me, if you are fully aware of the value of time as regards your immortal spirit. I cant say that I advise you to laugh, but if you are punished, and I warned you, that can be no business of mine. So I fold up my arms, and leave you to fate—may it deal very kindly with you! The trinity winds up with me, as you may have surmised, and I certainly would'nt be at the fag end but for civility to you. This selfsacrificing spirit will be the ruin of me! I am occupied principally with a cold just now, and the dear creature *will* have so much attention that my time slips away amazingly. It has heard *so* much of New Englanders, of their kind attentions to strangers, that it's come all the way from the Alps to determine the truth of the tale—it says the half was'nt told it, and I begin to be afraid it was'nt. Only think, came all the way from that distant Switzerland to find what was the truth! Neither husband—protector—nor friend accompanied it, and so utter a state of loneliness gives friends if nothing else. You are dying of curiosity, let me arrange that pillow to make your exit easier! I stayed at home all Saturday afternoon, and treated some disagreable people who insisted upon calling here as tolerably as I could—when evening shades began to fall, I turned upon my heel, and walked. Attracted by the gaiety visible in the street I still kept walking till a little creature pounced upon a thin shawl I wore, and commenced riding—I stopped, and begged the creature to alight, as I was fatigued already, and quite unable to assist others. It would'nt get down, and commenced talking to itself—"cant be New England—must have made some mistake, disappointed in my reception, dont agree with accounts, Oh what a world of deception, and fraud—Marm, will [you] tell me the name of this country—it's Asia Minor, is'nt it. I intended to stop in New England." By this time I was so completely exhausted that I made no farther effort to rid me of my load, and travelled home at a moderate jog, paying no attention whatever to it, got into the house, threw off both bonnet, and shawl, and out flew my tormentor, and putting both arms around my neck began to kiss me immoderately, and express so much love, it completely bewildered me. Since then it has slept in my bed, eaten from my plate, lived with me everywhere, and will tag me through life for all I know. I think I'll wake first, and get out of bed, and leave it, but early, or late, it is dressed before me, and sits on the side of the bed looking right in my face with such a comical expression it almost makes me laugh in spite of myself. I cant call it interesting, but it certainly *is* curious—has two peculiarities which would quite win your heart, a huge pocket-handkerchief, and a very red nose. The first seems so very *abundant,* it gives you the idea of independence, and prosperity in business. The last brings up the "jovial bowl,[2] my boys," and such an association's worth the having. If it *ever* gets tired of *me,* I will forward it to *you*— you would love it for *my* sake, if not for it's own, it will tell you some queer stories about me—how I sneezed so loud one night that the family thought the last trump[3] was sounding, and climbed into the currant-bushes to get out of the way—how the

[2]A bowl of alcoholic punch.
[3]Trumpet.

rest of the people arrayed in long night-gowns folded their arms, and were waiting—but this is a wicked story, it can tell some *better* ones. Now my dear friend, let me tell you that these last thoughts are fictions—vain imaginations to lead astray foolish young women. They are flowers of speech, they both *make,* and *tell* deliberate falsehoods, avoid them as the snake, and turn aside as from the *Bottle* snake, and I dont *think* you will be harmed. Honestly tho', a snake bite is a serious matter, and there cant be too much said, or done about it. The big serpent bites the deepest, and we get so accustomed to it's bites that we dont mind about them. "Verily I say unto you fear *him.*" . . .

Your very sincere, and *wicked* friend,
Emily E Dickinson.

Letter 31

To Austin Dickinson

17 October 1851

. . . How glad I am you are well—you must try hard to be careful and not get sick again. I hope you will be better than ever you were in your life when you come home *this time,* for it never seemed so long since we have seen you. I thank you for such a long letter, and yet if I might choose, *the next* should be a longer. I think a letter just about *three days* long would make me happier than any other kind of one—if you please, dated at Boston, but thanks be to our Father, you may conclude it *here.* Everything has changed since my other letter—the doors are shut this morning, and all the kitchen wall is covered with chilly flies who are trying to warm themselves—poor things, they do not understand that there are no summer mornings remaining to them and me and they have a bewildered air which is really very droll, did'nt one feel *sorry* for them. You would say t'was a gloomy morning if you were sitting here—the frost has been severe and the few lingering leaves seem anxious to be going and wrap their faded cloaks more closely about them as if to shield them from the chilly northeast wind. The earth looks like some poor old lady who by dint of pains has bloomed e'en till *now,* yet in a forgetful moment a few silver hairs from out her cap come stealing, and she tucks them back so hastily and thinks nobody *sees.* The cows are going to pasture and little boys with their hands in their pockets are whistling to try to keep warm. Dont think that the sky will frown so the day when you come home! She will smile and look happy, and be full of sunshine *then*—and even *should* she frown upon her child returning, there is *another* sky ever serene and fair, and there is *another* sunshine, tho' it be darkness there—never mind faded forests, Austin, never mind silent fields—*here* is a little forest whose leaf is ever green, here is a *brighter* garden, where not a frost has been, in its unfading flowers I hear the bright bee hum, prithee, my Brother, into *my* garden come![1]

Your very aff
Sister.

Letter 58

[1]Note the poem embedded in this letter.

To Susan Gilbert (Dickinson)

late April 1852

So sweet and still, and Thee, Oh Susie, what need I more, to make my heaven whole?

Sweet Hour, blessed Hour, to carry me to you, and to bring you back to me, long enough to snatch one kiss, and whisper Good bye, again.

I have thought of it all day, Susie, and I fear of but little else, and when I was gone to meeting it filled my mind so full, I could not find a *chink* to put the worthy pastor; when he said "Our Heavenly Father," I said "Oh Darling Sue"; when he read the 100th Psalm, I kept saying your precious letter all over to myself, and Susie, when they sang—it would have made you laugh to hear one little voice, piping to the departed. I made up words and kept singing how I loved you, and you had gone, while all the rest of the choir were singing Hallelujahs. I presume nobody heard me, because I sang *so small,* but it was a kind of a comfort to think I might put them out, singing of you. I a'nt there this afternoon, tho', because I am here, writing a little letter to my dear Sue, and I am very happy. I think of ten weeks—Dear One, and I think of love, and you, and my heart grows full and warm, and my breath stands still. The sun does'nt shine at all, but I can feel a sunshine stealing into my soul and making it all summer, and every thorn, a *rose.* And I pray that such summer's sun shine on my Absent One, and cause her bird to sing!

You have been happy, Susie, and now are sad—and the whole world seems lone; but it wont be so always, "some days *must* be dark and dreary"! You wont cry any more, will you, Susie, for my father will be your father, and my home will be your home, and where you go, I will go, and we will lie side by side in the kirkyard.

I have parents on earth, dear Susie, but your's are in the skies, and I have an earthly fireside, but you have one above, and you have a "Father in Heaven," where I have *none*—and *sister* in heaven, and I know they love you dearly, and think of you every day.

Oh I wish I had half so many dear friends as you in heaven—I could'nt spare them now—but to know they had got there safely, and should suffer nevermore—Dear Susie! . . .

Emilie—

Letter 88

To Susan Gilbert (Dickinson)

27 June 1852

. . . Susie, will you indeed come home next Saturday, and be my own again, and kiss me as you used to? Shall I indeed behold you, not "darkly, but face to face" or am I *fancying* so, and dreaming blessed dreams from which the day will wake me? I hope for you so much, and feel so eager for you, feel that I *cannot* wait, feel that *now* I must have you—that the expectation once more to see your face again, makes me feel hot and feverish, and my heart beats so fast—I go to sleep at night, and the first thing I know, I am sitting there wide awake, and clasping my hands tightly, and thinking of next Saturday, and "never a bit" of you.

Sometimes I must have Saturday before tomorrow comes, and I wonder if it w'd make any difference with God, to give it to me *today,* and I'd let him have Monday, to make him a Saturday; and then I feel so funnily, and wish the precious day would'nt come quite so soon, till I could know how to feel, and get my thoughts ready for it.

Why, Susie, it seems to me as if my absent Lover was coming home so soon— and my heart must be so busy, making ready for him.

While the minister this morning was giving an account of the Roman Catholic system, and announcing several facts which were usually startling, I was trying to make up my mind wh' of the two was prettiest to go and welcome *you* in, my fawn colored dress, or my blue dress. Just as I had decided by all means to wear the blue, down came the minister's fist with a terrible rap on the counter, and Susie, it scared me so, I hav'nt got over it yet, but I'm glad I reached a conclusion! I walked home from meeting with Mattie, and *incidentally* quite, something was said of you, and I think one of us remarked that you would be here next Sunday; well—Susie— what it was *I* dont presume to know, but my gaiters seemed to leave me, and I seemed to move on wings—and I move on wings now, Susie, on wings as white as snow, and as bright as the summer sunshine—because I am with you, and so few short days, you are with me at home. Be patient then, my Sister, for the hours will haste away, and Oh *so* soon! Susie, I write most hastily, and very carelessly too, for it is time for me to get the supper, and my mother is gone and besides, my darling, so near I seem to you, that I *disdain* this pen, and wait for a *warmer* language. With Vinnie's love, and my love, I am once more

Your Emilie—

Letter 96

To Samuel Bowles

about February 1861

Dear friend.[1]

You remember the little "Meeting"—we held for you—last spring? We met again—Saturday—'Twas May—when we "adjourned"—but then Adjourns—are all—The meetings wore alike—Mr Bowles—The Topic—did not tire us—so we chose no new—We voted to remember you—so long as both should live—including Immortality. To count you as ourselves—except sometimes more tenderly—as now—when you are ill—and we—the haler of the two—and so I bring the Bond— we sign so many times—for you to read, when Chaos comes—or Treason—or Decay—still witnessing for Morning.

We hope—it is a tri-Hope—composed of Vinnie's—Sue's—and mine—that you took no more pain—riding in the sleigh.

---

[1]Samuel Bowles was the editor of the *Springfield Daily Republican,* Amherst's local daily, a politically liberal and nationally influential newspaper. Bowles and his wife were lifelong friends of Dickinson's. Some scholars argue that Dickinson was in love with Bowles, and for some he is a likely candidate for the "Master" whose identity has never been revealed.

We hope our joy to see you—gave of it's own degree—to you—We pray for your new health—the prayer that goes not down—when they shut the church—We offer you our cups—stintless—as to the Bee—the Lily, her new Liquors—

> Would you like summer? Taste of our's.
> Spices? Buy here!
> Ill! We have berries, for the parching!
> Weary! Furloughs of down!
> Perplexed! Estates of violet trouble ne'er looked on!
> Captive! We bring reprieve of roses!
> Fainting! Flasks of air!
> Even for Death, a fairy medicine—
> But, which is it, sir?

Emily
Letter 229

To recipient unknown

about 1861

Master.[1]

If you saw a bullet hit a Bird—and he told you he was'nt shot—you might weep at his courtesy, but you would certainly doubt his word.

One drop more from the gash that stains your Daisy's bosom—then would you *believe?* Thomas' faith in Anatomy, was stronger than his faith in faith.[2] God made me—[Sir] Master—I did'nt be—myself. I dont know how it was done. He built the heart in me—Bye and bye it outgrew me—and like the little mother—with the big child—I got tired holding him. I heard of a thing called "Redemption"—which rested men and women. You remember I asked you for it—you gave me something else. I forgot the Redemption [in the Redeemed—I did'nt tell you for a long time, but I knew you had altered me—I] and was tired—no more—[so dear did this stranger become that were it, or my breath—the Alternative—I had tossed the fellow away with a smile.] I am older—tonight, Master—but the love is the same—so are the moon and the crescent. If it had been God's will that I might breathe where you breathed—and find the place—myself—at night—if I (can) never forget that I am not with you—and that sorrow and frost are nearer than I—if I wish with a might I cannot repress—that mine were the Queen's place—the love of the Plantagenet[3] is my only apology—To come nearer than presbyteries[4]—and nearer than the new Coat—that the Tailor made—the prank of the Heart at play on the

---

[1]Drafts of three letters to "Master" were among Dickinson's papers when she died. It is not known if final copies were ever made and sent. She refers to herself as "Daisy" in two of the letters.

[2]Doubting Thomas (John 20:25) required physical proof of Christ's resurrection.

[3]The family name of a line of English sovereigns is used here perhaps as a generic term for royalty.

[4]Priests or ruling elders of a church.

Heart—in holy Holiday—is forbidden me—You make me say it over—I fear you laugh—when I do not see—[but] "Chillon"[5] is not funny. Have you the Heart in your breast—Sir—is it set like mine—a little to the left—has it the misgiving—if it wake in the night—perchance—itself to it—a timbrel is it—itself to it a tune?

These things are [reverent] holy, Sir, I touch them [reverently] hallowed, but persons who pray—dare remark [our] "Father"! You say I do not tell you all— Daisy confessed—and denied not.

Vesuvius dont talk—Etna—dont—[Thy] one of them—said a syllable—a thousand years ago, and Pompeii heard it, and hid forever—[6] She could'nt look the world in the face, afterward—I suppose—Bashfull Pompeii! "Tell you of the want"—you know what a leech is, dont you—and [remember that] Daisy's arm is small—and you have felt the horizon hav'nt you—and did the sea—never come so close as to make you dance?

I dont know what you can do for it—thank you—Master—but if I had the Beard on my cheek—like you—and you—had Daisy's petals—and you cared so for me—what would become of you? Could you forget me in fight, or flight—or the foreign land? Could'nt Carlo,[7] and you and I walk in the meadows an hour—and nobody care but the Bobolink—and *his*—a *silver* scruple? I used to think when I died—I could see you—so I died as fast as I could—but the "Corporation"[8] are going Heaven too so [Eternity] wont be sequestered—now [at all]—Say I may wait for you—say I need go with no stranger to the to me—untried [country] fold—I waited a long time—Master—but I can wait more—wait till my hazel hair is dappled—and you carry the cane—then I can look at my watch—and if the Day is too far declined—we can take the chances [of] for Heaven—What would you do with me if I came "in white?"[9] Have you the little chest to put the Alive—in?

I want to see you more—Sir—than all I wish for in this world—and the wish— altered a little—will be my only one—for the skies.

Could you come to New England—[this summer—could] would you come to Amherst—Would you like to come—Master?

[Would it do harm—yet we both fear God—] Would Daisy disappoint you— no—she would'nt—Sir—it were comfort forever—just to look in your face, while you looked in mine—then I could play in the woods till Dark—till you take me where Sundown cannot find us—and the true keep coming—till the town is full. [Will you tell me if you will?]

I did'nt think to tell you, you did'nt come to me "in white," nor ever told me why,

> No Rose, yet felt myself a'bloom,
> No Bird—yet rode in Ether.

Letter 233

---

[5]A castle prison in a poem by Lord Byron.
[6]Vesuvius and Etna are volcanoes in Italy and Sicily. Vesuvius, erupting, destroyed the town of Pompeii in the first century A.D.
[7]Dickinson's dog.
[8]Ruling elders, perhaps of a church.

[9]This may mean dressed in white, a color Dickinson associated with immortality. Late in her life she is said to have dressed exclusively in white. Or here she may be associating white with the paper on which she presented herself in letters and poems.

To Susan Gilbert Dickinson

date uncertain

Dear Sue—[1]

Your praise is good—to me—because I *know* it *knows*—and *suppose*—it *means*—
    Could I make you and Austin—proud—sometime—a great way off—'twould give me taller feet—
    Here is a crumb—for the "Ring dove"—and a spray for *his Nest,*[2] a little while ago—*just*—*"Sue."*

Emily.

Letter 238

To T.W. Higginson

15 April 1862

Mr Higginson,[1]

Are you too deeply occupied to say if my Verse is alive?
    The Mind is so near itself—it cannot see, distinctly—and I have none to ask—
    Should you think it breathed—and had you the leisure to tell me, I should feel quick gratitude—
    If I make the mistake—that you dared to tell me—would give me sincerer honor—toward you—
    I enclose my name—asking you, if you please—Sir—to tell me what is true?
    That you will not betray me—it is needless to ask—since Honor is it's own pawn—

Letter 260

To T.W. Higginson

25 April 1862

Mr Higginson,

Your kindness claimed earlier gratitude—but I was ill—and write today, from my pillow.

---

[1]This note is part of an exchange of remarks about "Safe in their Alabaster Chambers," Poem J. 238. Susan seems to have suggested changes in the original version of the poem. After Dickinson sent the next version, Susan praised the first verse but wrote that she was still not suited with the second. So Dickinson sent a third version along with this note. The exchange reveals how exacting a critic Susan could be and how willing Dickinson was to please her.

[2]"Ring dove" was the term Susan had used for her new baby. Dickinson probably sent a "crumb" from her kitchen and a "spray" from her garden with the note.

[1]Dickinson wrote this unsigned letter to Higginson after reading his "Letter to a Young Contributor" in the *Atlantic Monthly,* April, 1862. She enclosed a card with her signature and four poems. The correspondence developed into a friendship which lasted a lifetime.

Thank you for the surgery[1]—it was not so painful as I supposed. I bring you others[2]—as you ask—though they might not differ—

While my thought is undressed—I can make the distinction, but when I put them in the Gown—they look alike, and numb.[3]

You asked how old I was? I made no verse—but one or two—until this winter—Sir—

I had a terror—since September—I could tell to none—and so I sing, as the Boy does by the Burying Ground—because I am afraid—[4]You inquire my Books—For Poets—I have Keats—and Mr and Mrs Browning. For Prose—Mr Ruskin—Sir Thomas Browne—and the Revelations.[5] I went to school—but in your manner of the phrase—had no education. When a little Girl, I had a friend, who taught me Immortality—but venturing too near, himself—he never returned—Soon after, my Tutor, died—and for several years, my Lexicon—was my only companion—Then I found one more—but he was not contented I be his scholar—so he left the Land.[6]

You ask of my Companions Hills—Sir—and the Sundown—and a Dog—large as myself, that my Father bought me—They are better than Beings—because they know—but do not tell—and the noise in the Pool, at Noon—excels my Piano. I have a Brother and Sister—My Mother does not care for thought—and Father, too busy with his Briefs[7]—to notice what we do—He buys me many Books—but begs me not to read them—because he fears they joggle the Mind. They are religious—except me—and address an Eclipse, every morning—whom they call their "Father." But I fear my story fatigues you—I would like to learn—Could you tell me how to grow—or is it unconveyed—like Melody—or Witchcraft?

You speak of Mr Whitman—I never read his Book—but was told that he was disgraceful—[8]

I read Miss Prescott's "Circumstance," but it followed me, in the Dark—so I avoided her—[9]

Two Editors of Journals came to my Father's House, this winter—and asked

---

[1]Perhaps cuts in poems suggested by Higginson.

[2]More poems.

[3]The imagery of "thought" "undressed" and "in the Gown" is unclear, but probably refers to Higginson's previous letter or to his "Letter to a Young Contributor."

[4]There has been much critical speculation on "the terror since September." Biographers have suggested a spiritual crisis, fear of blindness due to an acute eye problem, an emotional breakdown the result of abandonment by someone Dickinson loved. The exact nature of the "terror" cannot be determined.

[5]Dickinson lists five English writers: three nineteenth-century poets, a nineteenth-century art critic, a seventeenth-century prose writer; and the last book of the Bible.

[6]None of these—the "friend," the "Tutor," the one who "left the Land"—can be positively identified.

[7]Legal documents.

[8]Walt Whitman's Leaves of Grass was first published in 1855. Readers were shocked by the poet's descriptions of his passions and appetites. The innovative appearance of the poetry with its unconventional punctuation may have prompted Higginson to ask if Dickinson had read Whitman. He seems to be looking for stylistic influences.

[9]Harriet Prescott Spofford's "Circumstance," published in the Atlantic Monthly in May, 1860, is a terrifying story of a woman held hostage "... in a tree by a beast which is pacified only when she sings to him." See Volume 2 of this anthology.

me for my Mind—and when I asked them "Why," they said I was penurious—and they, would use it for the World—[10]

I could not weigh myself—Myself—

My size felt small—to me—I read your Chapters in the Atlantic—and experienced honor for you—I was sure you would not reject a confiding question—

Is this—Sir—what you asked me to tell you?

Your friend,
E—Dickinson.

Letter 261

To T.W. Higginson

7 June 1862

Dear friend.

Your letter gave no Drunkenness, because I tasted Rum before—Domingo comes but once[1]—yet I have had few pleasures so deep as your opinion, and if I tried to thank you, my tears would block my tongue—

My dying Tutor told me that he would like to live till I had been a poet, but Death was much of Mob as I could master—then—And when far afterward—a sudden light on Orchards, or a new fashion in the wind troubled my attention—I felt a palsy, here—the Verses just relieve—

Your second letter surprised me, and for a moment, swung—I had not supposed it. Your first—gave no dishonor, because the True—are not ashamed—I thanked you for your justice—but could not drop the Bells whose jingling cooled my Tramp—Perhaps the Balm, seemed better, because you bled me, first.

I smile when you suggest that I delay "to publish"—that being foreign to my thought, as Firmament to Fin—

If fame belonged to me, I could not escape her—if she did not, the longest day would pass me on the chase—and the approbation of my Dog, would forsake me—then—My Barefoot-Rank is better—

You think my gait "spasmodic"—I am in danger—Sir—

You think me "uncontrolled"[2]—I have no Tribunal.[3]

Would you have time to be the "friend" you should think I need? I have a little shape—it would not crowd your Desk—nor make much Racket as the Mouse, that dents your Galleries—

---

[10]Dr. Holland and Samuel Bowles, both of the *Springfield Daily Republican,* appear to have urged Dickinson to publish. By this time, Bowles had published one of her poems, probably without her permission.

[1]Santo Domingo is the capital of the rum-producing Dominican Republic. Dickinson is saying that she had tasted praise before, and that the first taste is like no other.

[2]Dickinson is quoting Higginson who apparently was describing rhythms and phrasing in the poems.

[3]A position from which to judge herself and pronounce her own sentence. It is likely that Dickinson is being ironic. There is no indication that she ever adopted any of Higginson's suggested changes.

If I might bring you what I do—not so frequent to trouble you—and ask you if I told it clear—'twould be control, to me—

The Sailor cannot see the North—but knows the Needle[4] can—

The "hand you stretch me in the Dark," I put mine in, and turn away—I have no Saxon,[5] now—

> As if I asked a common Alms,
> And in my wondering hand
> A Stranger pressed a Kingdom,
> And I, bewildered, stand—
> As if I asked the Orient[6]
> Had it for me a Morn—
> And it should lift it's purple Dikes,
> And shatter me with Dawn!

But, will you be my Preceptor, Mr Higginson?

> Your friend
> E Dickinson—

> Letter 265

To T.W. Higginson

July 1862

Could you believe me—without? I had no portrait, now,[1] but am small, like the Wren, and my Hair is bold, like the Chestnut Bur—and my eyes, like the Sherry in the Glass, that the Guest leaves—Would this do just as well?

It often alarms Father—He says Death might occur, and he has Molds of all the rest—but has no Mold of me, but I noticed the Quick wore off those things, in a few days, and forestall the dishonor—You will think no caprice of me—

You said "Dark." I know the Butterfly—and the Lizard—and the Orchis—

Are not those *your* Countrymen?

I am happy to be your scholar, and will deserve the kindness, I cannot repay.

If you truly consent, I recite, now—

Will you tell me my fault, frankly as to yourself, for I had rather wince, than die. Men do not call the surgeon, to commend—the Bone, but to set it, Sir, and fracture within, is more critical. And for this, Preceptor, I shall bring you—Obedience—the Blossom from my Garden, and every gratitude I know. Perhaps you smile at me. I could not stop for that—My Business is Circumference—An ignorance, not of Customs, but if caught with the Dawn—or the Sunset see me—My-

---

[4]Needle of a compass.
[5]The English language. Dickinson is saying that she has no words.
[6]The East.
[1]Here, and in the following paragraph, she explains that she has no photograph of herself to send to Higginson. At age ten a portrait had been painted of the three Dickinson children, and when she was about sixteen, her daguerrotype was made, but, as she tells Higginson, she had never had a photograph taken. This appears to have been the case throughout her life since there are no verified photographs or portraits of Dickinson as an adult.

self the only Kangaroo among the Beauty, Sir, if you please, it afflicts me, and I thought that instruction would take it away.

Because you have much business, beside the growth of me—you will appoint, yourself, how often I shall come—without your inconvenience. And if at any time—you regret you received me, or I prove a different fabric to that you supposed—you must banish me—

When I state myself, as the Representative of the Verse—it does not mean—me—but a supposed person. . . .

To thank you, baffles me. Are you perfectly powerful? Had I a pleasure you had not, I could delight to bring it.

Your Scholar

Letter 268

To Mrs. J.G. Holland

early May 1866

Dear Sister,

After you went, a low wind warbled through the house like a spacious bird, making it high but lonely. When you had gone the love came. I supposed it would. The supper of the heart is when the guest has gone.

Shame is so intrinsic in a strong affection we must all experience Adam's reticence. I suppose the street that the lover travels is thenceforth divine, incapable of turnpike aims.

That you be with me annuls fear and I await Commencement[1] with merry resignation. Smaller than David you clothe me with extreme Goliath.

Friday I tasted life. It was a vast morsel. A circus passed the house—still I feel the red in my mind though the drums are out.

The book you mention, I have not met. Thank you for tenderness.

The lawn is full of south and the odors tangle, and I hear today for the first the river in the tree.

You mentioned spring's delaying—I blamed her for the opposite. I would eat evanescence slowly.

Vinnie is deeply afflicted in the death of her dappled cat, though I convince her it is immortal which assists her some. Mother resumes lettuce, involving my transgression—suggestive of yourself, however, which endears disgrace.

"House" is being "cleaned." I prefer pestilence. That is more classic and less fell. . . .

Emily.

Letter 318

[1]Commencement exercises at Amherst College.

To Susan Gilbert Dickinson

about 1870

Oh Matchless Earth—We underrate the chance to dwell in Thee

Letter 347

To Susan Gilbert Dickinson

about 1870

We meet no Stranger but Ourself.

Letter 348

To T.W. Higginson

1876

Nature is a Haunted House—but Art—a House that tries to be haunted.

Letter 459A

To Otis P. Lord [rough draft]

about 1878

My lovely Salem smiles at me I seek his Face so often—but I am past disguises (have dropped—) (have done with guises—)[1]

I confess that I love him—I rejoice that I love him—I thank the maker of Heaven and Earth that gave him me to love—the exultation floods me—I can not find my channel—The Creek turned Sea at thoughts of thee—will you punish it— [turn I] involuntary Bankruptcy as the Debtors say. Could that be a Crime—How could that be crime—Incarcerate me in yourself—that will punish me—Threading with you this lovely maze which is not Life or Death tho it has the intangibleness of one and the flush of the other waking for your sake on Day made magical with [before] you before I went to sleep—What pretty phrase—we went to sleep as if it were a country—let us make it one—we could (will) make it one, my native Land—my Darling come oh *be* a patriot now—Love is a patriot now Gave her life for its (its) country Has it meaning now—Oh nation of the soul thou hast thy freedom now

Letter 559

---

[1]Dickinson drafted letters as she did poems— writing several words or versions of a line or phrase, and then making a choice. This is a rough copy of a piece of a letter to Judge Otis Lord, a friend of the Dickinson family.

Dickinson corresponded with Lord, who lived in Salem, Massachusetts, from about 1878 to his death in 1884. Her letters indicate that the two were in love with each other.

To Susan Gilbert Dickinson

about 1878

I must wait a few Days before seeing you—You are too momentous. But remember it is idolatry, not indifference.

Emily.

Letter 581

To Susan Gilbert Dickinson

early October 1883

Dear Sue—

The Vision of Immortal Life has been fulfilled—[1]

How simply at the last the Fathom comes! The Passenger and not the Sea, we find surprises us—

Gilbert rejoiced in Secrets—

His Life was panting with them—With what menace of Light he cried "Dont tell, Aunt Emily"! Now my ascended Playmate must instruct *me.* Show us, prattling Preceptor, but the way to thee!

He knew no niggard movement—His Life was full of Boon—The Playthings of the Dervish were not so wild as his—

No crescent was this Creature—He traveled from the Full—

Such soar, but never set—

I see him in the Star, and meet his sweet velocity in everything that flies—His Life was like the Bugle, which winds itself away, his Elegy an echo—his Requiem ecstasy—

Dawn and Meridian in one.

Wherefore would he wait, wronged only of Night, which he left for us—

Without a speculation, our little Ajax[2] spans the whole—

> Pass to thy Rendezvous of Light,
> Pangless except for us—
> Who slowly ford the Mystery
> Which thou hast leaped across!

Emily.

Letter 868

---

[1]Gilbert, Susan and Austin's youngest child, died of typhoid fever on October 5, 1883.

[2]A hero of Greek mythology known for his size and his courage.

To Susan Gilbert Dickinson

about 1884

Morning[1]
might come
by Accident—
Sister—
Night comes
by Event—
To believe the
final line of
the Card[2] would
foreclose Faith—
Faith is *Doubt*—

Sister—
Show me
Eternity—and
I will show
you Memory—
Both in one
package lain
And lifted
back again—

Be Sue—while
I am Emily—
Be next—what
you have ever
been—Infinity—

Letter 912

---

[1]Because Thomas Johnson inaccurately represents margins, line breaks, and spaces between apparent stanzas, we reprint here an exact copy of the original manuscript of what can be seen as a letter-poem.
[2]"The final line of the Card" may refer to a standard Victorian greeting card or to a message written on a card. Or the card may be a playing card or a fortune-telling card. By metaphorical extension the "Card" may refer to the Bible.